The Pervert in the Hills

The Pervert in the Hills

J P HOLZER

**Sophie Toscan du Plantier murdered
23.12.1996**

'We'll never have the truth': death of suspect Ian Bailey floors family of French film-maker

Sophie Toscan du Plantier's relatives tell of Irish murder case, years of seeking justice and hope cold case inquiry will continue

📷 The body of Sophie Toscan du Plantier was found badly beaten outsider her holiday home in County Cork in December 1996. Photograph: Family Handout/PA

Ian Bailey was convicted for the murder of Sophie on 31.05.2019. Died 21.01.2024

| | News | Sport | Fabulous | TV | Showbiz | Money | Travel |

SOPHIE TOSCAN DU PLANTIER

| Courts | Crime | Features | Murderers And Serial Killers | Print Features |

COLD CASE I met drunk wife-beater Ian Bailey and left convinced he was a calculated killer

IN the end, Ian Bailey's drinking was suicidal. He was supposed to get in shape

Contents

Foreword

I had hoped Ian Bailey would write this foreword. I offered him the opportunity to do so.

A cheeky request: November 16^{th,} 2023 (email to Ian Bailey)

Hi mate,
Delighted that you have not found any errors or raised any objections regarding the chapter outline on your false accusations threats and bullying re Ff. I am pretty thorough and have a good database. Given you did say all that filth to her will you apologise? Or is the John Wayne State of mind about telling sick sexual lies about a woman and then gutlessly hiding from the truth - I must have missed that John Wayne movie. Likewise, as a Christian you should make a genuine apology to Ff otherwise one has to conclude you are lying about being Christian, what is it to be?

I do have a copy of your mealy mouthed 'apology' to JG after you got it completely wrong about my ID. The truth is, you actually tried to blame unknown unnamed people for your appalling conduct. I know at that time I was running rings around you, exposing so many of your weaknesses. However, that is no excuse for not being man enough to face up.

As I said last time if you want me stop just say the word and the emails will stop.

The cheeky request is to ask you to write the foreword for my book - Pervert in the Hills. I could give you up to 500 words. Just think of how many times you can call me arseholser, turd, gobshyte ! You can say I am a crooked cop, a Dublin businessman who stalked you, a guy in Sheffield with domestic violence convictions, a criminal psychopath. Or make up something really new. If it helps feel free to attribute it to a 'troll hunter' or some unnamed tech person. Or something you learned about me in an Australian newspaper article that no longer exists. i don't mind. You can fill your boots. It may be a means of catharsis. You could look at it as me helping you to purge and purify yourself. I would invite you to do it as a poem, but that would be ridiculous.

Pip pip
JPH

He did not take up my generous offer.

Why *Pervert in the Hills*

Pervert was written expecting Bailey to be alive. It is not something created once he had died. This will be seen when I share emails I sent to Bailey in the later months of 2023 through to the day he died. He was in no doubt that I was going to expose his lying and incompetence. Moreover he knew that I would address the significant evidence that he hated women and had a lifelong sexual interest in underage girls.

The last full paragraph I ever wrote to him was on the day he died:

> *"I think next I will send you the details of your on the record sexual interest in underage girls in the 1990s right through last year. We can both agree I am a fair minded man who follows the facts. If I have made a factual error let me know. and I will make changes. Be assured that the image of the 'naughty girl' masturbating that you so liked and the dick pic of your unimpressive penis will be redacted for taste."*

The pervert aspect may be self-explanatory but why *Pervert in the Hills?* On January 2nd, 2000 Professor John Montague wrote a brilliant article for the New Yorker magazine about the murder of Sophie Toscan du Plantier. For a brief time, Bailey had been Montague's gardener in West Cork. The title of the article was A Devil in the Hills. This influenced the name of this book. It will show the perverted nature of the man who murdered Sophie.

Go brách

The content of this book is for adults 18+ only.
[There are many tweets, articles, emails, and messages quoted in this book. In all cases the original spellings are included even if incorrect. The only redacting is for explicit imagery, the privacy of individuals, and foul language.]

Introduction

This is a true story

Have you ever had one of those days when you go to a Farmer's market for some locally produced cheese, cured meats, and freshly baked bread and then come away with a book of appalling poetry written by a convicted murderer, who is soon threatening to kill you and keeps calling you a turd, then years later the man eventually drops dead an hour after you send him a mocking email?
    I have.
    This is what happened.

JPH

CHAPTER 1

Me and the monster

21.04.2018

After visiting Baltimore in Co Cork to see where the barbary pirates emptied the village by taking over two hundred slaves in 1631, I took the short journey to Skibbereen. I visited the Farmer's market on the Saturday before I returned to England. There was always a delightful array of stalls. The fresh produce was tempting as were the craft stalls. On that Saturday I also bought a photograph of Gougane Barra, a famous beauty spot and religious site, and a couple of second-hand books. It was increasingly impossible to ignore one incongruous stall with an even more incongruous stall holder.

Tacked on at the end of long rows of professionally constructed and presented stalls was what looked like a flimsy trestle table. A slight breeze would probably send it crashing. The table and the floor around it were covered in small potted plants. There were two non-plant items on the table. The first was a dissertation with the word Policing or Police on the cover. The second was a pile of thin paperback books, which were for sale.

The stallholder was an imposing figure when observed from a distance. He was 6' 3" with broad shoulders, wearing a long dark coat, even though the day was mild, and a large cowboy hat. On closer inspection, his attire appeared preposterous. He was a man who wanted to stand out, he wanted to be seen. That would account for the dissertation that I assumed was his, and the poetry he was selling. He had given this some thought. He stood out all right. However, he lacked the self-awareness to appreciate what people would see beyond the grand gestures.

The gestures – and in later years the big talk – smacked of desperation. The act of a mediocrity who thinks he ought to have been something. Such people always bring to mind the Brando lines in On the Waterfront, "You don't understand. I coulda had class. I coulda been a contender. I coulda been somebody, instead of a bum, which is what I am, let's face it." I did not know whether this man could amount to much. I did know he looked weird and was flogging plants off a wonky table. Close up he looked tired and unhealthy. Heavy bags growing under his eyes, a lined face, the bulbous hint of a 'drinker's nose.' He looked to have poor dental hygiene. He liked to stand remarkably close when speaking and his breath could have been better. I thought he was in his late sixties and ravaged by heavy drinking and possibly drugs.

Once he learned we were from the North of England and heard our accents he was all over us. That was his 'in.' There followed a monologue from the stallholder, it was as if he breathed through his ears and did not need to pause to draw breath. He had no interest in selling us any of his wares. Instead, he took great pleasure in talking about himself.

The stallholder first announced that he was from Manchester. This struck me as odd because he did not have a hint of a Mancunian accent. He did not have any accent at all. Someone, his parents? his school? his elocution teacher? had trained any dialect out of him. He said he had been a journalist in England but had given it all up twenty or so years ago and made a new start in West Cork.

He appeared overconfident in the way narcissists can be, though he might have had talents and achievements that justified his cockiness. [Spoiler alert – later I learned there were no talents or sustainable achievements.]

The first time I heard the phrase 'blow in' was courtesy of the talkative man. He said he was a gardener, a poet, and a woodworker. If we needed to know anything about West Cork he could give us a steer. We bought a few plants and a paperback book. He signed the book, we made our exit. We laughed. Happy to free ourselves from this unctuous and boring man.

Poetry book

Driving home from Skibbereen my wife read a few verses from some of his poems. It was impossible to get through a whole poem without laughing. We were not surprised to see that the book was self-published and there was no reference to there being an editor. There is nothing wrong with self-publishing but this book could be filed under 'vanity project.' When introducing poems, the author would write some biographical details. One that made no sense to me was:

> "Then out of a clear blue sky came the equivalent of a small nuclear warhead and for many years my life was overtaken by events."

I had no idea what the author meant by this and cared even less. The book was thrown into a bag of books that would be taken back to the UK. In normal circumstances, it may have been read once more and then taken down to a local charity shop. It was not a keeper. And that would have been the end of it. Given that his plants and poetry were lousy and he was weird we would give him a wide berth if we saw him again at the market.

29.04.2018 Sunday Times India Knight

> "I'm gripped by a true-crime podcast about a suspected murderer living in plain view in Ireland – and you will be too"

ST India Knight article 29.04.2018

The first Sunday back in the UK I got the usual Sunday
papers including the Sunday Times. In the ST magazine was
India Knight's column. It was always worth a look but this
one was unique. She was writing about the gripping West
Cork podcast. The column was headed:" I'm gripped by
a true-crime podcast about a suspected murderer living in
plain view in Ireland – and you will be too"

The article explained how the podcast had grabbed
Knight's attention. A story of the brutal murder of Sophie

Toscan du Plantier on December 23rd, 1996. Alone at her remote cottage, she had been savagely beaten. The murderer had still not been caught twenty-two years later. The victim's family continues to be tortured by Sophie's death and their inability to get justice for her. (Appendix 1)

Yet there was a prime suspect. Who many, including the police, believed to be the murderer. An Englishman called Ian Bailey. As Knight described this Englishman I had the creeping realisation that she was referring to the man I had met in the Skibbereen market just over a week earlier. She wrote: "And it remains the place where Bailey, mills about, has a cake and pizza stall at the market, and sells a book of his appalling poetry, " An Englishman milling about in a market selling dreadful poetry. Who else could it be? Surely there could not be two men like that. Knight added:

> "Bailey cannot stop talking to them….He frequently refers to himself in the third person….He can't get enough of himself."

> "….One assumes that Bailey was a man who likes a certain amount of notoriety, likes to be in the limelight, and likes a bit of self-publicity."

I knew it was the weird man in Skibbereen market but I still checked. I emptied the bag of books I had taken back to the UK and there it was, The West Cork Way by Ian Bailey. Signed by the man himself.

The autographed book

The quickest of Google searches brought up countless articles about the murder of Sophie Toscan du Plantier in 1996. She was a French documentary maker with a second home, a cottage in a remote location, in West Cork. The murderer had repeatedly beaten her about the head with a large concrete block. There were additional injuries, It had been a crazed attack. The prime suspect was Ian Bailey.

Just a couple of articles into the case and it was obvious why Bailey had soon become a suspect. He gave An Garda Síochána (AGS) a false alibi for his whereabouts at the time of Sophie's murder. AGS is Ireland's National Police and

Security Service. The false alibi was initially confirmed by his partner Jules Thomas.

The 1996 murder was the 'small nuclear warhead'. But was Bailey a victim or was he the warhead?.

I was hooked.

From that moment on I devoured material about the case. Excellent journalism by Barry Roche, Senan Molony, and Ralph Riegal plus the West Cork podcast. At that time there were two books on the case. Death in December: The Story of Sophie Toscan Du Plantier by Michael Sheridan and L'affaire Sophie Toscan du Plantier: Un déni de justice by J-A Bloc. The later book is only available in French. Thank heavens for free online translation services.

There was no lack of information on this case. There was an Office of the Director of Public Prosecutions (DPP) report in 2003 that concluded Bailey should not go to trial, and the proceeds of two civil cases that Bailey lost. One case was his attempt to sue newspapers and the other was effectively suing AGS. There were several reports such as the McAndrew Report 2007, the Fennelly Commission 2017, and the GSOC (Garda Síochána Ombudsman Commission) report 2018. In 2019 he had been tried in absentia in France and found guilty of the murder. The Irish courts decided that he would not be extradited to France. From 2020 to 2022 there were no less than four further books published on the case and two large-scale documentaries on Sky Crime and Netflix.

On June 10th, 2021, Bailey posted his first tweet and his first output on social media. As he was to say many times that post ended his 'social media virginity.' He liked to sexualise issues. Often his copy resembled the output of some coarse unfunny wannabe 'Carry On' script writer. The man claimed to be a legal academic, a poet, and an inestimable investigative journalist. I assumed he would master social media and demonstrate intelligence and wit. This is what he tweeted when I started working on this book. He was hopeless. He never was an overwhelming success. But I am sure he thought he was.

Ian Kenneth Bailey BCL, LLB, LLM (UCC)
@IanKennethBail1

Did anybody here of the excremention of Fascist Pyhsco Dudearelist JPHolzer of Yorkshire Anti Neurotic Feaces... 😂 😂 😂

11:16 PM · Jan 6, 2024 · **435** Views

This was the output of a man who said he had been a successful journalist. He rarely missed an opportunity to tell people he had three law degrees. He invented the self-description of legal academic. He wanted people to believe he was a legal expert and a highly intelligent man. Finally, he craved recognition as a serious poet. Read that tweet again. Feel free to read many or all of his tweets. Whatever he claimed to be this is what he produced. His 'shining glory' was to be his podcast. That had less foul language but also showed the man for what he was. By looking at his media output and in particular his social media engagement it became possible to see the real man, in plain sight.

When he decided to engage on social media it was an opportunity for me to see how the man operated. Was he the fearsome and intimidating man he would have us believe? Perhaps he would use these platforms to make a coherent case supporting his claims of innocence.

At that point in time he had been found guilty of the murder of Sophie. There was a mountain of circumstantial evidence to support that conviction. His supporters tried to claim that circumstantial convictions were somehow inherently unsafe. This was, and is, pure nonsense. They implied that without DNA a conviction would be untenable. They failed to understand that DNA evidence is circumstantial evidence and that until well into the 1980s was not part of any criminal investigation.. I soon learned that facts, details, and testing evidence were of little interest to Bailey and his small band of active supporters.

As little more than an 'amateur detective,' I could not expect to solve the case. However, in time I would do some original analysis that showed his involvement in the murder. I decided that what I could do was take a look at his output and see if any patterns could be detected.

And so it began. It was a hoot.

Bailey and the discussion of his crimes on social media

The normal way to discuss the details of a criminal case is for people to raise topics or specific issues. Contributors would then put forward a hypothesis and produce evidence that either supports or falsifies it. This is done in an environment of reasoned discourse and thoughtfulness. What I found when I looked at Bailey was ' a whole different ball of wax'.

The sleep of reason doth make monsters

He and his closest allies did not engage in this normal way. There was a whole new Baileyite approach created in the 'master's' image. In terms of the case, detail was replaced by slogans. The mouthing of small soundbites or simple emotive tropes had replaced rational, reasoned discussion.

That would be bad enough if it were limited to a few ill-informed people. However, it appeared that every single person in his camp was using the same limited playbook. Sadly it was much worse than this. he and the other people pushing the slogans did not stop there. When challenged on the facts they would quickly opt for one or more of three strategies. They might

- Lie
- Insult
- Threaten (including bullying)

He was a pathological liar. He would lie about the case and the people involved in it. He presented false narratives as facts. He went further. He would spread vicious lies about people who challenged his point of view or conduct. As we shall see this included claiming people had committed serious crimes. He loved to insult people just for the sake of it. Central to this was making rude and disparaging comments about a person's appearance. He would claim people had many types of psychological or psychiatric problems. On top of all that he would say that people were uncouth and unintelligent. At the time of his arrest and later he would claim Police officers were uneducated and unintelligent. He claimed that many of the people who said he had confessed were incapable of understanding irony. This was typical Bailey. Lies and insults were bad enough but it got even worse.

There would be excessive bullying and threatening of those people who did not comply with his point of view, this will be particularly evident in the chapter on his misogyny. He wanted to dox people, threatened to name them, and spread lies about them. Doxing is the process of searching for and publishing private or identifying information about a particular individual on the internet, typically with malicious intent. It is done without the consent of the person being doxed. Rather than block or ignore a person the doxer targets them. By revealing private information the aim is to damage people and threaten them. We see below that some of Bailey's supporters have been very threatening. He used doxing as a weapon. He wanted to spread his bile with their employers, He wanted them to worry about him turning up in their communities.

He also asked his followers to confront his adversaries in the street. He went so far as to threaten to kill me. I did not take this threat too seriously as his preference was for severely beating and murdering small and frail women, rather than being violent with men who might retaliate.

There was also another threat of violence that he had in his arsenal. He had several accounts, clearly run by a much smaller number of people, based in Northern Ireland. Some of these people would make hideous and vile threats. They would seek to dox the children, siblings, and partners of people who were doing nothing more than suggesting that Bailey may have murdered Sophie. Implicit in this behaviour was the message; we know who you are, who your close family is and we know where you live. These account holders would threaten to turn up at people's homes and worse.

In the message below the phrase 'remove someone from the planet' is a clear death threat being issued from a now-defunct account. The actual name of the account holder or his wife was unclear. He knew what it meant when he said these people were tracking someone. He knew the sorts of threats they would be issuing. This illustrated the malevolent nature of him and his most ardent followers. Challenging them may result in threats of humiliation and harm. Little wonder I saw pleasant people scared away from discussing the man's potential guilt.

You know this is being tracked not only by AGS but friends in West Belfast... 😊😊😊

11:37 pm

I know your friends in Belfast very well
Wink wink
You're played again 😆😆😆

You old fool

😂😂😂😂😂

#BantheHuntNI #TeamFoxNI #FBPE #F... @EdwardFox... · Feb 26 ···
if my wife's name as much as passes your lips ever again i will personally remove you from this planet. i know your identity now Mr
. Be very careful. your stalking and harassment has gone way over the limit. You want to start a war? You got one

As in many situations when dealing with Bailey, the darkness of who and what he was, would be interspersed with humour, laughing at him of course.

Once identified, the sheer one-eyed approach to the crime by him and his supporters became a cause of laughter. They had some predictable ways of responding when discussing the murder.

The weird sorts of discussions you could have with Baileyites

Let's discuss whether Bailey did it (normal people)

He didn't do it (Baileyites)

We could look at the evidence

it was a hitman

which book have you read about the case?

There was no DNA

Pick a book and we can discuss it

The Gards lost the gate with all the DNA

There is an article by Senan Molony that explains it was not lost. Perhaps you would like to discuss one of the documentaries?

The bottom line is AGS fitted up Bailey. It wasn't him.

The GSOC report and the 2014 trial did not find the fitting up of Bailey

They were part of the fit up.

The French court found Bailey to have done it, no fit up there

The French trial was a kangaroo court.

What evidence are you basing your overall point of you on?

I've been giving you evidence!

But nothing coherent

Says you, you arrogant bastard. ..

And on and on it would go spiralling into threats

To an outsider, it may be hard to believe that adults would lie and hurl insults at people for wanting to take a reasoned approach. These lies could lead to bullying and possibly threats of harm. This was exactly what was going on. By seeing what he was doing it was possible to map out a way of challenging him, and his cronies.

The key approaches would be:

1. Keep pushing on the case evidence and testing evidence
2. Call out his many and varied lies and keep pressing him for the truth and proof of what he says
3. He liked dishing out the insults, see if he could take it. Play a little hardball
4. Expose his threats and bullying stand up to them, and call him out

It would be fair to say Bailey did not like what happened next.

How the monster liked to address me

← **Tweet**

 Ian Kenneth Bailey
@IanKennethBail1   ...

So The Arse Holzer will meet his demise... SATURDAY 12 NOON...

12:47 am · 8 Apr 2022 · Twitter for Android

Ian Kenneth Bailey BCL, LLB, LLM (UCC)
@IanKennethBail1   ...

Hello friends, fans, followers and the very trolls. It is my suspicion that
the Arch Troll JPArseholzer is on the loose in Ireland...He is clearly a
dangerous lunatic so if anybody wants to go after him and challenge him
to reveal his true identity I will meet him and teach him

8:04 PM · Apr 7, 2022

Ian Kenneth Bailey   ...
@IanKennethBail1

Im being libebelled and slhanderedered by an Anglo Nonse...Whose
looking for a Sicko Confrontation Here in Ireland...We will deal with Such
Langers As HISTORICALLY DONE...Come out and meet...Fight like a
Man...Not that Ye Can...Langer JPArseHolzer...Ye feckin Mocka

10:15 pm · 23 Feb 2023 · **1,190** Views

Ian Kenneth Bailey @IanKennethBail1 · 1h
ARS HOLZER..COME OUT AND FIGHT ME IF YE NONCE, IF YE DARE
TOMORROW IN SKIBEREEN MARKET...WEAR MULTIPLE UNDER ...ALL
EYES WILL BE ON YE ...LANGEROUS SHYTE...CANNOT WAIT..YE BRIT
PIECE OF USELESS EXSCREMENTIAL SCUM 😁 😁 😁

Ian Kenneth Bailey BCL, LLB, LLM (UCC)   ...
@IanKennethBail1

What a pare of pathetic human exceemwyties are Arseholzer and Fart
😂 😂 😂 yer both a paie of danferoua sex starved pervs 😂 😂 😂 😂
...so sad

12:38 am · 6 Apr 2023 · **931** Views

Ian Kenneth Bailey
@IanKennethBail1

···

I NOTE AN ANONYMOUS ZENAPHOBIC ONANISTIC PSYCHOPATHETIC TROLL ..JPHOLZER..OF NORTH ENGLAND IS RANTING ON..SPOUTING VITRIOLIC NONSENSE ABOUT ME AGAIN...WHAT A SADDO..A REET NUTTER..HE SHOULD SEEK TREATMENT 😂 😂 😂

6:45 PM · Mar 9, 2023 · **628** Views

3 Likes

CHAPTER 2

Bailey's sexual interest in young girls

Paedophile: someone who is sexually attracted to children.

One of the most disturbing aspects of Bailey's diaries and journals was his sexual interest in underage females. He had stated that he had used pornography since the age of twelve. This is a very young age for a boy to be using this material. He also stated that he preferred hardcore porn. This is sexually explicit and may extend to illegal sexual practices including adults having sex with children.

He wrote in his diaries "I can quite clearly verify that exposure to erotica and porn does head to the mind being taken over by lustful thoughts. On other matters I feel calm as well although I dwell on sex much of the time – my mind is often full of the most graphic acts of sex. Intercourse, oral and anal. I love anal sex with a person." A man who masturbated excessively from twelve years old wrote those words approximately twenty-five years later. That is a very long time to have an extreme sexual orientation. He admits he was obsessed with sex. There is also another factor here. He writes as if he has no control over himself, and that he is not responsible for his actions. He chooses to seek out and use extreme pornography. His choice. He chooses to use pornography so much that his thoughts are taken over by sex. Here is a man who has disturbing desires claiming it was not his fault. This was the same rationale when his brutal domestic violence was exposed. In that case, it was not 'him' it was 'the drink.' He tried to pass the buck for his violence onto alcohol and not his behaviour.

When it came to the crunch, despite him blaming porn and booze for his unacceptable behaviour, he did not stop using either of them. Ultimately, he would always continue with his foul behaviour and seek to make excuses for it. There is the old saying, 'it is easier to ask for forgiveness than permission'. He sought neither. As a narcissistic psychopath, he did what he wanted.

In his book Killing Sophie, Elio Malocco publicised Bailey's obsession with hardcore pornography, frequent masturbation, and underage girls. It was the latter that caused many of his most active supporters to turn against him. One such person was Alisa Rose (Amanda Large). She had at one time run a high-profile PR campaign for Bailey. She stopped working with him in September 2021. Six months later she felt compelled to make a statement on social media about the man.

Alisa Rose statement 20.03.22

I ran a campaign for Ian Bailey. I stepped away quietly months ago due to professional issues with him. **I was ill when revelations came out re sex with minors. I was refused access to these files. From hospital I replied that I no longer supported him but made no official statement."**

"I regret this campaign misery, broken agreements, embarrassment. It is a decision I can't change & will be debated in the public domain."

To her credit, she spoke up on this issue when it would have been easier in many ways to remain silent. Rose was not alone in walking away from him. The man's continued interest in underage girls since her statement supports her judgment call.

He was a former journalist and wannabe poet. These are occupations in which the precise use of language is paramount. He aimed to write exactly what he meant, with precision. After the murder of Sophie, he tried to hide his writings from AGS because he did not want them to see what he thought privately. At one point he writes about watching pornography late into the night. It is a sickening observation.

Everybody asleep. Just watched a [illegible]. Highlight was three males into one little girl.

He refers to a little girl. Not a petite or diminutive woman. A little girl is a child, almost certainly prepubescent. If three adult males are having intercourse and performing other sexual acts with a child then they are paedophiles and the child is being raped and sexually abused. For normal people this is sickening, for him, it was the highlight of his evening. A child was being raped and it aroused him. He felt compelled to make a record of it. Most likely he was masturbating while watching her being used. Little wonder he did not want his degenerate filth in the public domain. His focus was on his pleasure. He was completely indifferent to the abuse of the little girl. There is no empathy for the child. Her suffering is okay if it gives him sexual pleasure. What a guy.

A second entry in his writings switches from pornography to wanting to have sex with a 14-year-old girl living in the same house. The child in question was the daughter of the woman with whom he was living. He is sexually interested in her and her similarly-aged friends.

> ...sexual feelings towards her. Fortunately to date my conditioning has prevented me from over dwelling on such feelings. Yet I have and no doubt will fantasize about the taking of a young one and her friends. I just find them so attractive. Any man would.

The sexual interest in prepubescent little girls is called paedophilia. When the interest is in 14 year olds it is Hebephilia. That indicates a strong sexual interest by adults in pubescent children in early adolescence, typically ages 11–14. In civilised countries and cultures these girls fall below the legal age of consent. A third category is Ephebophilia, which relates to girls who are 15-19 years old. In many countries including Ireland, the age of consent is found at 16 or 17. This means that ephebophiles may also be inclined towards sex with underage girls.

A telling comment by Bailey in that journal entry is "ANY MAN WOULD". This reveals an assumption that all men are sexually interested in children. It attempts to normalise a perverse orientation. This worldview is common among those people interested in sex with children. They like to pretend everyone thinks as they do and conclude what they do is mainstream. A man thinking that sex with children is mainstream is a constant threat to them.

In late 1996 and 1997, the police in Co Cork were collecting statements concerning the murder of Sophie Toscan du Plantier. In doing so they collected further information about Bailey and an underage child. In a statement, Caroline Leftwick explained that there was a birthday party in Skibbereen for a young woman, Maire. Bailey and Jules Thomas were in attendance. He was aged thirty-nine at the time and was flirting with Maire. Also, in attendance was fifteen-year-old Carly Leftwick. That night on the way home Carly told her mother she had gone to the toilet and when she was returning to the party through a utility room she met Bailey. He picked her up by the ribs and lifted her to his level and asked her to wrap her legs around him. She was startled, and upset by what happened and refused. This had angered Mrs Leftwick. She stated, "Had I been aware of this incident at the party I would have confronted Ian Bailey." Fair to say many people would have more than confronted him. Some might have called AGS others might have thumped him.

When the DPP reviewed all the evidence for the Sophie Toscan du Plantier murder case they attributed his behaviour to him being 'flirtatious. A 39-year-old man grabs a girl, without her consent, under her ribs and close to her breasts. He lifts her without her consent and then invites her to wrap her legs around him. This later action is also an invitation for her to press her upper body into him. And someone at the DPP thought that was flirting. God help us! Despite the behaviours of the man and the strange conclusions of the DPP what is evident is he thought it okay to grab a child and make sexual advances. People interested in the murder case will notice how when drunk he may be inclined to grab hold of a woman he finds attractive. It is crude and coarse behaviour with violent intent and limited interest in consent.

The child being raped in a video, a sexual interest in the 14-year-old daughter of his partner, and grabbing a 15-year-old are all examples of inappropriate sexual behaviour concerning female children. This all happened 25-plus years ago. In the absence of psychological or drug therapies, people with these sexual preferences will likely continue to have them. I decided to analyse his social media output. Would a man like him still have an interest in underage girls? I was mortified by the dark tendencies and perverse attitudes that I uncovered.

Social Media

Initially, there were a few warning signs that his interest in underage girls had not waned. At first, this was in a comparatively 'mild form.' He showed an interest in a Twitter account called @katie53001. That account had multiple photographs of girls who looked like they were in their early teens but dressed in a more adult fashion.

Some of the images had the girls posing while scantily clad. There was no nudity or semi-nudity. All the girls, and they were girls, not women, appeared to be under sixteen. He was effusive in his praise. He used terms like gorgeous, charming, and enigmatic. A man in his mid-sixties feeling the need to look through these images and comment upon them was a little odd, but certainly not illegal. Not long after he started showing an interest in the account it was suspended for violating Twitter's rules. Presumably for the inappropriate sexualising of children. It remains suspended.

If this had been the full extent of his activities then it might have been seen as distasteful. It did show how he was keen to look at underage girls. That was concerning. However, this was just the beginning. The later developments were alarming.

"Vagzilla"

In May 2022 I was sent several dozen DMs exchanged between Bailey and an account with the improbable name of Vagzilla. It appeared to be the account of a schoolgirl saying she was 15 years old. This is two years under the age of consent in Ireland and fifty years younger than him.

I was not sure whether this was a genuine approach by a young girl, some form of extortion ploy, the work of online paedophile hunters, or catfishing. What was intriguing was his excited and explicit response. All his responses were being made to this self-declared, inexperienced 15-year-old child.

I'm a 15 year old schoolgirl never been touched 🙊 I need a man with experience to educate me sexually

After just a few exchanges of DMs (DM, a private direct message between two people on Twitter), he started to arrange a meeting with the child. He established when her final term finished, he gave her a cover story to explain their meeting and he went as far as suggesting she bring a friend. The sexual DMs were unrelenting. He wrote about his erections, whether she was a 'squirter,' referred to oral sex regularly, and inserting a courgette in her for sexual purposes. He wanted her to sit on his face. If this were not bad enough he sent her a photograph of his penis or as he called it, his 'thirsty mouth' or 'pinky.' He was desperate to get feedback on the photograph from the girl.

This was all in line with his earlier sexual interest in the 14-year-old and lifting up the 15-year-old. It demonstrated the crude immature 'seduction technique' being used by this lecherous man with a yearning for girls. Below are just a few of the Twitter DMs he was sending several times a day.

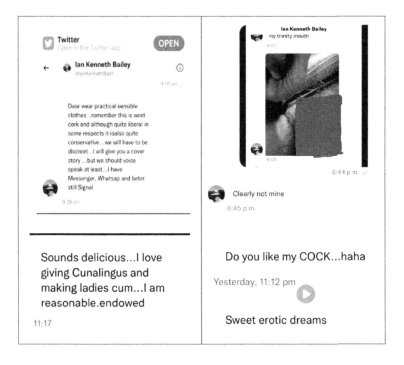

> Well how me eating.your
> yoni while pleasing and
> pleasuring you with a
> suitably sized organic
> courgette..
>
> 15:26
>
> didnot tell me if you like
> photograph on me little pinky

[On thepervertinthehills.co.uk website many more examples of Bailey's social media output will be posted]

Later, when confronted with the explicit photograph he said it was not his penis. He said no more. Yet it was beyond doubt a picture sent by him. It is almost as if he thought sending the photo of someone else's penis to Vagzilla was okay. If it was not his penis then why did he refer to it as '**my** thirsty mouth' and why did he follow up the photograph with 'did you like **my** cock' and ' **me** little pinky.' This is not an untypical response by him. A front-on denial despite the overwhelming evidence. A denial no one believed.

Bailey is called out on his grooming behaviour

When faced with what he had done. Bailey denied it. A woman on Twitter challenged him. His response did not so much deny it nor confirm it. Instead, he attempted to bully and threaten the woman into silence. This will be spelled out in greater detail in the chapter on misogyny. Bailey started telling vile lies about the woman and threatening her with getting those lies to her community, her employer, the local newspapers, and AGS. There it was again. Lying and threatening was something I would see him repeat many times including times when the lies and threats were aimed at me.

That woman and others would not back down. His bluff had been called. The woman would not give way. At this point, he claimed he had been hacked. He gave no further details – there weren't any. He was asked if he had reported the 'hacking' to Twitter, but he did not reply. If the 'hacking' related to underage sex he could also have told the Police. However, one of his DMs showed that he did not think Vagzilla was involved with the alleged hacking. He thought her to be real, a child and he continued to want sex with her. He feared that the hacking might expose his interest in the girl. He asked her to delete all her DMs and then move to a different platform where they could continue to plan their 'tryst'.

DM Bailey to Vagzilla

Hi think somebody hacked my twitter....I. deleted all our chats...suggest you do same immediatley...best switch to Whatsapp

 Consider this urgent...best

Furthermore, given the content being referred to was the grooming of a schoolgirl he was asked if he had reported the

'miscreant' to AGS. Once again he refused to answer the question. It seemed he would not take any action to help AGS to capture a potential paedophile. If his tale were true he could clear his name and do something positive for the people of Ireland. He chose not to. It was evident that his DMs with Vagzilla were real to him.

There was no substance to his suggestion that hacking led to the paedophilic DMs being sent from his account. He knew it. He knew that he was exchanging DMs with Vagzilla. He believed he may have been hacked and the hacker might have exposed his attempt to groom the schoolgirl. He thought the schoolgirl was real.

This confirms he was exchanging the grooming DMs with Vagzilla and he wanted it to continue. Little wonder he would not go to AGS. If they went through his social media output they would find the vile DMs and the photo of his penis. Heaven knows what other things they may have uncovered if they looked at his search history. In later months I challenged him to meet me and we could both go to Skibbereen AGS station and hand in our phones and computers so they could be examined. He declined. Is anyone surprised? In the aftermath of his death, the Police will discover the contents of his phone and computer.

The bullying, threats, denial, and hacker story had failed. So, Bailey came up with, drum roll, further lies. A regular default position for him was to blame me. The 'it was Holzer' position is based upon his paranoia. Was I Vagzilla?. Maybe I was the hacker or maybe I hypnotised him and made him send those DMs? All nonsense of course. I hoped he might have sued me re Vagzilla, he likes to sue people. He would have lost the case as I had played no part in his squalid communications.

Pathological liars just keep on lying. So, it was no surprise that he produced a further excuse. It was as if he just blurted out anything that came into his head with little thought about how a sane person may make sense of it.

His final effort to cover up his grooming behaviour was to claim it was a sex game with Vagzilla who he said was in her 20s. In this fiction, Bailey says it was the woman who asked him to treat her as if she was a fifteen-year-old schoolgirl. Bailey keeps tying himself in knots. If people were to, foolishly, believe his story then it meant he was only too happy to spend time and energy pretending he was an immature degenerate. What sort of normal man enthusiastically indulges in 'paedophilic sex games' with a complete stranger? The most likely answer is the man is not normal and he is interested in underage sex.

He did not have a single DM or communication supporting the older woman pretending to be a child excuse. Not one. For a man with three law degrees, he always appeared to be evidence-lite. Well, not so much lite as non-existent. A man who made a great show of being cautious with other people has no record of the alleged setting up of the game. He had no corroboration and he expected people to take his word for it. If these communications were being done with an adult in a role-playing game he could have said, 'We are both adults, playing a game.' Instead, he hurriedly asked Vagzilla to delete everything on Twitter and move to a different platform.

If it was a regrettable, role-play game between adults then why all the bullying, threats, and repeated lies? Why say it was a hacker if the truth was it was a woman in her 20s? Why claim it was me when it was apparently a 20-plus-year-old woman? It was nonsense. If he were telling the truth he could have asked Vagzilla for her copy of the communications. Instead, he did what pathological liars do. He lied some more. The man was drowning in his own lies.

There is an even bigger truth, a bigger insight into his mindset. The pattern of behaviour here appears almost hard-wired into his thinking. When his conduct is lamentable or shameful, even criminal he would always lie to cover it up. If the lie does not succeed in covering it up then he will produce a new lie. If that fails he may lie again. And on it goes. He continues even when his lies contradict each other. It resembled a compulsion. He appeared to give no thought to the fact that his false explanations are trackable and contradict each other. Those contradictions only go to expose his dishonesty. It is a strategy that never caused him to stop his unpleasant behaviour.

Bailey and the masturbating child
February 8th, 2023

On February 8th, 2023, Bailey posted a tweet that unequivocally demonstrated his sexual attitudes towards underage girls. He was commenting on a tweet that included a video approximately one and a half minutes long. It showed a child who looked to be aged between 11 and 13 years old. The girl danced a little and removed a few remaining clothes. Then she sat on a chair remarkably close to the camera, spread her legs wide apart, and masturbated.

Ian Bailey tweeted his comment about the child masturbating. There for all his 5,000-plus followers to see. He wrote "Yer a BEAUTIFUL NAUGHTY GIRL 😄😄😄

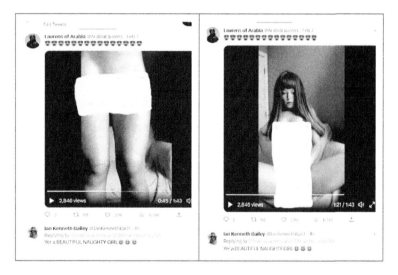

Almost thirty years after watching three men into one little girl he was commenting on a 'beautiful girl' masturbating in a video. Shortly you will see what happened when Bailey was challenged on Facebook about his liking of a child masturbating. His tweet remains on his timeline. The images, like those of the underage girls shown earlier, were removed by Twitter. The paedophilic account was closed down.

The daughter of his partner (14) the daughter of a friend (15) over twenty-five years ago and the 15-year-old Vagzilla recently. The little girl being raped by three men in the 90s and the child masturbating in a video in 2023, are both liked by Bailey. Nothing changes and all of it is shameful.

Ian Bailey and Manchester Artist on his interest in underage girls

In May 2023 as part of several weeks of discussions on a wide variety of topics on Facebook messenger, The Facebook account Manchester Artist, the account holder called Emms, took the opportunity to challenge Bailey's views on the murder of Sophie, his verbal attacks on women, his pathological lying, and his attitude to underage sex. The discussion about underage girls proved to be the most revealing. Manchester Artist raised the issue of the masturbating girl. he was asked why he liked the video. He freely states his opinions.

On the 26th of May in a series of messages, he made it clear what he thinks about child pornography. It is very revealing yet makes for bleak reading. The exchange started at 11.26 am, he was told that a UK author was planning an e-book for Kindle on him. Below we see reference to the tweet sent by Bailey on February 8th, 2023.

Via Facebook messenger Bailey is challenged about liking this child pornography. His first response is to claim this was all the creation of JP Holzer. Oh dear, we have been here before. One minute he would tell people he paid me no attention, the next he implied I was some sort of internet mastermind out to get him. 😂 As some people suggested, it appeared I had taken occupancy in his head. I would never do such a thing. While there may have been an abundance of space, the place would be too dark, too dirty, and alcohol sodden. He claimed there was no girl. It is pathetic and a typical response when he has been called out. If something was not there how could it be the creation of anyone? This is typical of him, offering completely contradictory explanations. He denied the facts and told lies to cover up what he had done. In his normal daily life, his approach would put a stop to him being challenged. Manchester Artist persisted and would not be fobbed off. The fact remained he was interested in a video of a child masturbating.

26/05/2023, 11:26

> Good morning Ian. Mark has seen the tweet and the girl, Says she is no more than 13. Hughes is going to put his book free of charge on kindle and ask people on social media to promote it. Mark says he will introduce me to Hman on the 10th but then he is done.

> Hughes told him hman has tweeted about the child in question. The photos are behind an advisory warning and the underdeveloped breasts / vagina and vagina being masturbated have been blocked out for reasons of decency. Will check out where they are, Emms x

There was no girl...it was a creation oh Holzers

> There was a girl and that is a provable lie Ian. You may have been out of your head at the time but It is real

26/05/2023, 12:17

Are you talking about a twitter picture?

Bailey denied the existence of anything at all, then, very quickly he referred to a 'picture'. He knew there was something there. He is not allowed to obfuscate on this issue. The detail is spelled out to him. It was a video and he knew it was a video, He had consistently posted videos on social media, and he knew the score.

He was provided with specific details that he could check on Twitter. There is also a reference to a picture of a young woman who he invited to sit on his face.

His next response is another fact-free meaningless ploy. he invents 'Vultures' and adds 'who have no real knowledge of reality'. This is gobbledygook. He liked a video of a child masturbating and commented favourably on it. That is a fact. No amount of waffle could change the truth.

Calling out a 66-year-old heavy drinker who likes watching a child masturbate is not 'clutching at straws'. It was a statement of fact. He was struggling. So, he tried another ploy. He changed the subject. He claimed he was spending the weekend with Jim Sheridan. The famous film director. His social media output showed no evidence of that. He lied to try and move away from the unpalatable truth. He was not allowed to do so here.

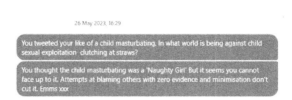

He was called out yet again. He does not like being challenged with facts. In this case, he got more facts than he could stomach.

So f...g what...girls post pix on twitter all the time...tis no crime

With his ploys utilised and proving unsuccessful we saw the real man. He is not being allowed to slip away from the truth. He no longer hides behind the façade of 'Holzer' or 'Vultures' or 'clutching at straws'. He conceded that the images and videos did exist. He goes on the attack. As more is put to him he cracks.

"So, f.....g what."

There we had it. He did not give a damn. Here speaks the narcissist. Here speaks the psychopath. Here speaks the pervert. To think there are people out there who supported this man.

"girls post pix on twitter all the time..tis no crime."
He was certainly correct to refer to girls. There are women, young women, and girls. The girls are not adults, they are underage. He thought children posting sexually explicit images was 'okay'. This rationale is common among people who want sex with underage children. They seek to normalise behaviour that is anything but normal. Children do not voluntarily produce a video of themselves masturbating and post it on social media. The sites and media accessed by Bailey may be full of such images. Maybe to him, it was normal.

Even if paedophilic photographs and videos are posted there is no reason to access them and even less reason to admire them. Yet this is exactly what he had done. He found the child porn, liked it and he wanted people to know he liked it. It brings to mind his comments about a little girl from decades earlier. If a child being abused gave him sexual pleasure, he did not care if she suffered.

This self-styled academic lawyer appeared to have concluded that getting a child to masturbate, filming it, and putting it out on social media - to lure perverts - is legal. He was wrong. He ignored the illegal child sexual exploitation that underpinned these videos as long as he got to watch a child masturbate. Or worse, see a child being raped. The Bailey supporters who defend this behaviour are likely to share his proclivities.

That is so much better Ian

Instead of the paranoia re Holzer or vulture talk or denying the facts you give a straight answer 👍

But it is perverse to gey hot and bothered about a child masturbating. Yes?

He was cornered. This was about him and the things he liked looking at. These were images and a video freely selected by him and liked by him. A child being forced to masturbate for a video is a crime and he knew it. Years ago, in his journals, he said a highlight had been watching three men have sex with a little girl. It's the same story. This is the real man. In his journals 30 years ago or in his social media output only months ago.

That was not all he said . There were more disturbing messages sent by him on that day.. He stated, 'I have a lot of underage girls coming on at me."

26 May 2023, 19:45

Joseph married Mary at 14...I have a lot of underage girls coming on at me...Im actually quite straight and proper...Im strict and proper with them...I am not Nabokkoff...two of my lady friends are 30 plus and my favourite is 46...I cannot help being a Babe Magnate 😜 😜 😜

One of the arguments frequently made by paedophiles is children are highly sexed and they instigate sexual activity with adults. If someone makes such a statement never leave them with or near children. We had seen him sexualising girls for decades and then he boldly stated they came onto him. It was not his fault, he had no choice, the children were coming onto him. He tried to pass the responsibility for his perversion onto children.

Let's dig into what this 66-year-old man had to say:

- "I have a lot of underage girls coming on at me."

As it stands the comment is sickening. When Bailey's assertion is unpicked it gets worse:

- "a lot"

Suggests that in his world he saw many underage girls who he insists were coming onto him. His comment is similar to what he said about many children happily masturbating on Twitter. 'The children' are being sexual so it was not his fault.

- "girls"

Refers to children not women.

- "underage"

How was this determined by Bailey? It's the guess of a creep. How young must a girl look for him to decide she is underage?

- "coming on at me"

What were these children doing for Bailey to decide they were coming onto him? What did this man consider to be a come-on? Was a child looking at him a come on? Was a child smiling a come on?

This was troubling. Not least because paedophiles will interpret what suits them and their sexual urges. What we knew for sure was that when Bailey saw underage girls he thought a lot of them were interested in him sexually. Sickening isn't it.

> Putting two Bailey comments together presents the image of a very disturbing worldview
>
> **"Any man would"**
>
> **"I have a lot of underage girls coming on at me."**
>
> A world where lots of underage girls come on to old men and any man would be keen to avail himself of such an opportunity

After writing about underage girls coming on to him Bailey concluded by saying he cannot help being a 'babe magnet' (magnate). Was he saying that includes him being incredibly attractive to female children? If so, that was depraved. He was saying it. He was depraved.

But you are a very bright man Ian. You must know that liking three men into one little girl and liking a video of a child masturbating is hard for most people to take. Have a good weekend,

Once again Bailey was challenged. He could no longer wriggle out from revealing his true self. He was asked about those people who were appalled by him watching a child being raped or forced to masturbate on film.

DILLIAGF ☺ ☺ ☺

Sorry DILLIAGAF

If you did not like his attitude to young girls then it is a case of DILLIAGAF (Do I Look Like I Actually Give A F***). There you have it. Ian Bailey's attitude to underage sex. The unvarnished truth. He liked it and he did not care what people thought. He did not give a f*** about people who oppose paedophilia. When daughters, granddaughters, nieces, or other female children looked at the weird drunk in the local West Cork market with his thinking stick and wearing his straw hat what was he seeing and thinking? He may well be deciding the child was putting out to him! And he did not give a f*** what anyone thought.

This was Ian Bailey. His thoughts and words could not be clearer. For decades the man had an abiding sexual interest in little girls.

CHAPTER 3

Bailey and women

Misogynist:
a person who dislikes, despises, or is strongly prejudiced against women

In chapter two there were many examples of Bailey believing female children exist for his sexual gratification. Along with murdering women the raping of female children ranks highest in the way a man can abuse a female. In this chapter, you will learn about his violence towards women and see how his misogyny became an almost daily activity. When they did not defer to him he disliked it, when they challenged him and he had no answers he loathed them. He would threaten women and bully them in many ways to get them to be quiet. If that failed he would call them a few more foul names and block them. And this is there for all to see online.

At the 2003-4 civil case, Justice Moran was scathing about Ian Bailey with women

At a 2003-4 civil trial, Ian Bailey sued five newspapers for linking him to the killing of Sophie. He lost all five cases. A highly experienced judge heard evidence for several weeks. All the evidence was tested by highly respected and thoroughly prepared barristers. At the end of the trial, the judge concluded:

> *"The question of violence towards women is a fact. What came across as a result of questions from Mr Gallagher is that Ms Thomas suffered three nasty assaults. Mr Bailey appeared in the District Court over one of those and received a suspended sentence. Mr Bailey says that when he was violent, it takes place domestically [sic] and is a domestic problem. I deal with a lot of family law in this court. One rarely comes across instances of beatings. In this case we have three. Violence once would be unusual. Violence twice would be unusual. Three times is exceptional. The District Court gave a six-month suspended sentence because his partner said she forgave him. Otherwise, the District judge would have had no hesitation in imposing a custodial sentence. I certainly have no hesitation in describing Mr Bailey as a violent man and I think the defendants have no problem in describing him as violent towards women, plural."*

One of the most compelling witnesses at the trial was Peter Bielicki. When Bailey savagely beat Jules Thomas and refused to let her daughters get her to hospital they went to their neighbour Peter Bielicki for help. In court, he described what he found at the Thomas cottage.

"I could hear what I can only describe as animal sounds of terrible distress. Jules was curled up at the end of the bed in foetal position. Her hair was completely tousled and large

clumps of her hair were missing, she had clumps of hair in her hand and her eye was purple. It was huge; a pink fluid was dripping from it and her mouth was swollen. Her face had gouges on it, her right hand had bite marks on it. It was like the soul, the spirit, had gone out of her. It was the most appalling thing I have ever witnessed."

Bailey admits to repeated violence

In his diary writing about the May 1996 attack he wrote: *"of late since Easter I have on a number of occasions struck and abused my lover "*. In 1996 Easter Sunday was April 7th. He struck and abused Thomas on several occasions over a three- or four-week period. Yet in other evidence, he claimed that in his entire relationship with Thomas, there had been 'only' three violent episodes. He has also claimed that he was ashamed of his behaviour and would never repeat it.

On 18.08.2001 in the home of Jules Thomas there was yet another violent physical assault. Bailey disagreed with Thomas. The physically imposing man took it upon himself to hit the woman he 'loved', more than once, in her face with a crutch. She had a black eye and an inflamed cheekbone. There was bruising of the lip. Thomas had bruising to her arms and legs. No injuries were recorded on him. A very brutal beating for the woman.

The DPP report about the du Plantier case told us how he and Jules Thomas invited a young woman, who had been drinking at their cottage, to sleep over. She was provided with a bed in a studio over 200 metres from the cottage.

In the early hours of the morning, the woman was woken up when Bailey, naked, climbed into her bed and started touching her. She had consented to none of this. he only stopped when Thomas arrived and interceded.

Social media: Women who challenge Bailey's point of view

The brutal and cowardly attacks on women behind closed doors is a matter of fact as mentioned by Judge Moran. I was keen to see if his vileness would manifest itself on social media. [SPOILER ALERT: It did]. There is plenty of the foulest language, bullying, threats, and sickening sexual allegations. While his fast-deteriorating health reduced his physical threat, his nastiness when dealing with women who questioned him or challenged him went unabated.

Bailey and the C-word

When women got under his skin he liked to use the c–word and cheap schoolboy insults. When Sinead O'Connor wrote an excoriating article about him for the Independent in 2021 he did not reply with the measured response one might expect from the self-styled academic lawyer and journalist. He resorted to vulgarity and rudeness. On Twitter Bailey uses the C- word only as a means of insulting women who stood up to him or challenged his worldview. He also used highly sexualised language. He did so like an inadequate 14 or 15-year-old boy who is rebuffed by a young woman. Most women found his lack of any subtlety and awkwardness unattractive, so he calls them c***s. He thought himself a big tough man when in reality he confirmed his immaturity. Unable to attract attention for good reasons he would prance around banging his Bodhran, shouting his 'poetry' and using the c-word with glee. What an absolute catch! It all meant the same thing; he was an inadequate boy shouting look at me...ME ME ME! Not caring who got hurt when he behaved that way.

Ian Kenneth Bailey

@IanKennethBail1

Here's one to ponder...does anybody out there think the Cu****ss of Gobshytes is none other than Sister Sinead.... the reason I ask is that some of her language is remarkably similar to the torrent of abusive texts I received from the ranting ex reporter...IKBO

4.03pm 24 Aug 2021 Twitter for Android

Ian Kenneth Bailey

@IanKennethBail1

So in another interest twist. The one who calls herself the Cu***ss Bouvier or something like that is non other than Ku***ss Ms Toma xxxxxx who has been reported to AGS cybercrime unit...tbc

7.41pm 29 Sep 2021 Twitter for Android

Ian Kenneth Bailey

@IanKennethBail1

Replying to @countessbouvierr

Happy nua year Cu****s

9.10pm Jan 2 2022 Twitter for Android

The Twitter account @Countessbouvier, a person
called Toma and the musician Sinead O'Connor had
all in their way made it clear that they disagreed with
his actions, words, or character. For this reason, he
bundled them all together and swore in one of the worst
ways possible. He could not differentiate between three
very different women. This was not a surprise. Like any
prejudiced person, he was prone to lump a whole category
of people together and damn them all. He thought using
that C-word with women was funny. He thought his
vulgarity commendable. This goes to the essence of the
way this man thought about women.

Between May 30th and June 2nd, He directed at least 10
tweets at the Countess. In ten tweets he aimed the c-word
at her 7 times. He threatened to dox the Countess account.
Doxing is done without a person's permission. And it is done
with clear malicious intent. When there were followers of
Bailey who threatened to turn up at people's front doors and
threatened serious physical harm, then doxing became a

serious threat. He said he would name and shame her to her employer. She tweeted in a personal capacity. Furthermore, her only sin was to challenge him on matters of fact. Her involvement was not linked with her work. This was classic Bailey. When a woman challenged him, or got the better of him, he would swear, bully, and threaten her.

The journalists who were happy to give his latest scheme or outburst full coverage did not say a word about this bullying filth. They gave him a free pass. Thankfully a small group of people, mainly women, none of them wealthy or in positions of power nor journalists decided that they would not let him go unchallenged. The bullying thug had made a big mistake. He had underestimated a group of women with principles. This was not surprising as he was a man who knew nothing about being principled.

A libelous outburst by Bailey

While there has been much fun to be had at the expense of the crass stupidity and incompetence of the odious Bailey. His conduct concerning one woman on Twitter is a case study in lying, bullying, and threatening behaviour. It was also a case study of a brave woman who would be bloodied but unbowed by his efforts. After his 'best' efforts it was he who retreated with his tail between his legs. A woman had run rings around him and he knew it.

The book of Elio Malocco, Killing Sophie describes his sexual desire for female children. That should have been sufficient reason for all decent people to stop supporting, serving, or financing this man. If anyone was in any doubt of his misogyny they should take a look at the information below. The woman, Ff, had consistently challenged him on the facts of the case, challenged his lies, and poked fun at this pompous convicted murderer. Throughout April he had been frequently swearing, trying to dox people. failing to deter anyone and repeatedly telling outrageous lies. Ff held Bailey's feet to the fire and he was unable to make a cogent case to respond to her questions.

Challenging Bailey's attempts at grooming

The grooming activities of Bailey with Vagzilla became known to a small number of people. One immediately reported the information to AGS. Another Ff decided to call him out as described in chapter two. As we saw he had plenty of 'answers' all conflicting and none of them remotely believable. Ff pressed him hard, brushing off the sort of feeble excuses that he got away with in the past. He was being pinned down and outsmarted. He could not admit defeat. Instead, he produced a vile narrative. A series of salacious and baseless lies about Ff. He not only lied on his timeline he threatened her on several occasions via direct messages, he concocted a story that she had been a sex worker in Melbourne, Australia. She had been convicted for that sex work and deported from Australia back to Ireland. Take a look at the tweets below.

Ian Kenneth Bailey

@IanKennethBail1

So any regulars may note I wa savagely thralled last yer by a bunch of nameless faceless crazies…well I now know the identities of several including a certain B****** women who used several fake accounts.. all details going to AGS …TBC

10.24pm May 8, 2022 Twitter for Android

Ian Kenneth Bailey

@IanKennethBail1

F******* seems to have gone quiet for a while…. COVID? Or Fear Truth?

3.17am May 10, 2022 Twitter for Android

Ian Kenneth Bailey

@IanKennethBail1

So due to my background as a Sunday Times investigative journo I have come up with some interesting back gound on the lead trolls…Did u know for instance that ************** of ******* M**** who trades under name ********** was actually deported from Australia for importuning

3.03pm 11 May 2022 Twitter for Android

Needless to say, the woman had never worked in that industry. She had never been to Australia. These are the bizarre sex-based fictions that hard-drinking hovel dweller Bailey came up with rather than admit he was wrong, discuss like an adult, or block the person. He enjoyed abusing the woman. That is how he got his thrills. Threatening women was his lifetime default position. His behaviour on social media proved it.

Ian Kenneth Bailey

@IanKennethBail1

So the throlls have got their foundation wear in a right twist. ******** who in herreal life guise … *** of ******** was deported from Australia for breaking prostitution law… and the arch throll JP Arseholzer is a disgraced former UK policeman…you could not may this up.

9.59pm 11 May 2022 Twitter for Android

We end up with this man asserting that the woman was kicked out of Australia for breaking the prostitution law. He claimed to have been a Sunday Times journalist and had 3 law degrees yet seems incapable of checking the most basic of facts. When a person is making very serious allegations about someone in print they ought to thoroughly check their sources. Later, in the Shattered Lives podcast in 2023, he boasted about rigorously checking his facts (another lie).

Who were his sources for this crapulence? How many independent trusted sources did he rely upon? He never gave an indication that he checked anything. These tweets were bad enough but he was not content with mere lies. He sought to bully and threaten this woman through a series of nasty DMs.

Ian Bailey's Twitter DMs used to try and intimidate a woman who called him out about his grooming activities

Got copies of the ******** and West Mayo Papers…tell me if you like my reporting and more importantly the photographs of you…don't be shy now ********** ****** the Australian newspaper reports are interesting….best IKBO] 12/05/22, 2.22am	Hahaha…think you might need to replace your vibrator batteries and get the e lube going. I;m going to be coming yer Mayo way next week…poetry gig be in Westport…should be great craic 12/05/22, 2.57am [Reply "See you there big guy It will be a great laugh Not for you though ### 12/05/22, 2.58am]

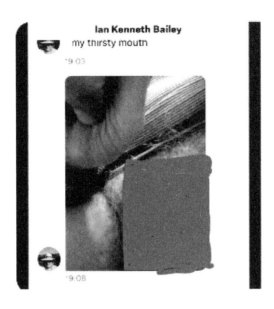

Ian Bailey's Twitter DMs used to try and intimidate a woman who called him out about his grooming activities

I know Joe has it…he's in for a big shock coming up.. and so are you if you don't stop being a nuisance. 11/05/22, 7.26pm	Caught him…he is a former policeman ejected from the force because of criminal behaviour…a bit like you in the land down under. 11/05/22, 9.21pm

Get copies of the B****** and W******** Papers, tell me if you like my reporting and more importantly the photographs of you ...don't be shy ******** ******* ...The Astralian newspaper reports are interesting....
best IKBO
12/05/22, 2.22am

Hahaha...think you might need to replace your vibrator batteries and get t he e lube going. I'm going to e coming yer Mayo way next week.. poetry gig be in Westport... should be great craic.
12/05/22, 2.57am

See you there big guy
It will be a great laugh
Not for you though 😩
12/05/22, 2.58am

Pog mot home
12/05/22. 1.58pm

Don't you remember Melbourne back in the eighties dear
12/05/22, 3.33pm

You even made the newspapers...if u like I will send you cutting...illegal Irish Sex worker Expelled

If it helps jog mamery I will post
12/05/22, 4.08pm

Go ahead
12/05/22, 4.18pm

Can you please provide proof of your very serious and libellous accusations
13/05/22, 1.03am
BAILEY BLOCKS

[Further examples of Bailey's threatening and foul DMs will be put on the www.thepervertinthehills.co.uk website]

Bailey made threats of making complaints to AGS. This had long been a favourite method of intimidation for him. He also threatened to spread his lies to the woman's employer to get her sacked. This cowardly behaviour is contemptible. In the exchanges, you will see that the woman politely requests that he take down his dishonest and damaging tweets. he replies 'Pog mo thome' (his 'Irish' version of 'up my arse'). This was the measure of the man. He went on to claim there were newspaper articles written about the faux conviction. He goes so far as to allude to a newspaper headline "Illegal Irish sex worker expelled". He offered to send her a cutting of an article. It is one thing to indulge himself in these weird fantasies it is another to make public allegations and make threats. At the end of this exchange, he adds 'If it helps jog your 'mamery; I will post'. He thinks she is vulnerable and unable to cope with one of his inadequate sexual jokes. Rather than back down the woman pushed back. She asked him several times to send or tweet the 'articles'. She knew there was not a grain of truth in what he was saying, She called his bluff and once again he was caught out. The requests for him to take down his lies were repeated and he did nothing. Let me make my point of view clear. Bailey the convicted murderer of Sophie Toscan du Plantier had doxed Ff and repeatedly lied about her. The lies are an attack on a woman who dares to challenge this miscreant. I offered him several thousand euros to provide us all with the articles. By this time he was wandering around Bantry like a tramp. He was cent-less. But he could not take up the offer of all that money because he was caught in his lies. He was now humiliating himself publicly in his desperation to impose his will. The more he tried the more he failed. The more desperate he became.

His behaviour was appalling.

To stop the woman from challenging his grooming behaviour he said she was -

- a sex worker
- convicted for sex work
- in Australia
- in Melbourne
- convicted in Australia
- deported from Australia
- the subject of actual articles supporting his accusations
- named in press cuttings re deportation in his possession

ALL LIES

To stop the woman from challenging his grooming behaviour he said

- he will publicise this wholly untrue story
- he will inform her employer
- he will report her to AGS
- he would be performing in her hometown soon
  (a threat)

ALL THREATS

The pattern of behaviour, in this case, is typical of him. Appalling behaviour followed by cover-up lies. Then more lies threats and bullying. In all these cases and many that are not mentioned in this book, we see when he is politely scrutinised by women he responds with a visceral overreaction.

CHAPTER 4

Getting to know him

Psychopath:

a personality disorder characterised by a lack of empathy, remorse, and conscience. Psychopaths are often manipulative, impulsive, and reckless. They may also be deceitful, dishonest, and have a grandiose sense of self-worth.

Narcissist:

an extremely self-centred person who has an exaggerated sense of self-importance

Malignant narcissism:

an extreme mix of narcissism, antisocial behaviour, aggression, and sadism. Grandiose, and always ready to raise hostility levels

It was clear from the beginning that Ian Bailey was narcissistic. This has been commented upon by the psychiatric and psychological experts who authored a major report on the French criminal trial. Also, a panel of four non-verbal communications experts reached a remarkably similar conclusion. Other criminal analysts share these points of view. Even a cursory analysis of him indicates that he is a very vain man with an extremely high sense of his importance and his talent.

He very quickly had several people, especially on Twitter, who actively supported him. Many tended to be aggressive to the point of bullying and threatening people. However, their arguments were weak. Both they and Bailey repeated a series of tired tropes about the case. After that, it was mainly lies, the foulest of language, threats, and vicious trolling.

Early on he did have the benefit of the support of at least two very bright women. One was Amanda Large a gifted public relations professional. She had come to the public's attention first as a Jack Sparrow impersonator and then more prominently as the woman who married the ghost of pirate. This later PR initiative got her a huge amount of national and international coverage. She had ran a campaign petition for Bailey claiming he was innocent and Justice for him would also mean Justice for Sophie. While it led to approximately 25,000 signatures for the petition it did little to show that Bailey was innocent. Some of the campaigners implied that the 2019 trial of Bailey in France was a show trial and that the justice system in France was that of a banana republic. That was tasteless and groundless.

Sophie's family had welcomed and agreed with the 2019 trial that found Bailey guilty of murder. They did not support the petition; they would never support what they saw as a cheap gimmick. To use Sophie's name and image in a campaign to support Bailey was insensitive and insulting. By September 2021 Amanda Large had moved on to other projects. To her credit she later went public with her condemnation of Bailey's sexual interest in underage girls (see chapter two) and made it clear that had she known about his perversion earlier she would never have helped Bailey with his campaign. He had lost one of his most formidable allies. As he was arrogant and always underrated women he did not appreciate what he had lost.

Soon after, a second woman who was probably his most intelligent activist withdrew her support following the revelations about Bailey's paedophilic tendencies. She also had long objected to his behaviour in public and in private. When she stopped supporting Bailey he put some vile comments about her on social media. Typical Bailey. From the point of view of the people who wanted to challenge him his loss of these two women was welcomed. From that moment on his social media output became chaotic and much more ineffective. The man was losing momentum but was failing to see it.

Decent people who wanted justice for Sophie and her family had concluded that he was almost certainly guilty and he should go on trial. Many of these people were 'driven' away from discussing the case by Bailey and his pals. A small number of people, mainly women, would not be bullied. But it was hard going for them. In most circumstances, like this, there would be a few newspapers and journalists who would lift their heads above the parapet and go toe to toe with Bailey and his yobs. This never happened until after the man died.

It was to be a roller coaster ride. Within a couple of years, he would threaten me with my demise more than once. I knew it was hot air but it showed the degree to which I had irritated him. By then I also knew that he preferred to hit women, not men. He asked his allegedly thousands of supporters to accost me in the street and pile on my Twitter account. Thankfully, the thousands claimed by him as supporters had little interest in their 'master.' He made a formal complaint about me to AGS alleging stalking. He could produce no evidence to support his allegations and the Police did not even need to speak to me. He was firing blanks and people could see it. He claimed he had made further complaints to the Police. This was one of his ploys when trying to intimidate people. It failed miserably. Having claimed he has made many complaints in Ireland and the UK he could not prove that he had done so. I have never been contacted by any officers as a result of these phantom complaints.

First things first

After a close look at Bailey and his fellow travellers, it was evident that he was weak. He always seemed to believe that people would accept what he said as truth. This is a theme in his prodigious lying output. In part, this was because he thought he was cleverer than everyone else. He saw himself as the master manipulator. The reality was that most intelligent and sane people had long seen him for the immoral waster he was.

He had to maintain this façade of being a puppet master. If he did not do so then he would be destroyed by the truth. It would crush him. The truth that he murdered Sophie, the truth that he was not too bright and a slow thinker. The truth is that he was a serial underachiever. The truth was that he was fur coat and no knickers. The truth is that he was ultimately weak and could be cut down to size.

I believed that the huge psychological effort of maintaining the myth of his existence would eventually grind him into the ground. While he was cock of the walk and others bought into his myth he was fine. If he were challenged it could all change. Under pressure, he would have to deploy huge amounts of psychological energy to maintain his status quo. There could be no knockout punch with Bailey. The approach would be to squeeze him day by day, cut by cut. At first, it would be imperceptible. He would continue to appear to be the ringmaster but below the surface, he would begin to struggle.

Each day he would get a little weaker and the pressure on him get a little stronger. He would have to work harder and harder to try and maintain his standing. A day or two of that is tiring. A month, six months two years of it, every single day is unsustainable for a guilty liar. I knew it was a battle of psychological attrition and he would inevitably lose. My challenge, and, later, that of others, was to stick with it and play the long game.

The tactics were simple. To incrementally turn the pressure up a notch, and weaken him a notch. With time there is a tipping point and the 'big beast of the jungle' would become easy prey.

In terms of the murder, the aim would be to keep confronting him with the weight of the evidence against him. Each time the pressure increases. It became harder for him to serve up the old failed arguments. He knew that failed arguments would be rebutted every time. As each bit of new evidence against him was found the pressure increased. When new insights were discovered in the old evidence, it was another way pressure was put on him. At the same time, his defences were being undermined. His tropes about the DPP or AGS corruption were taken apart piece by piece. The racist nonsense about the French legal system was exposed.

As time progressed the weight of the evidence used to support him becomes increasingly indefensible. The banality of the arguments becomes ever harder to sustain. He thought he was waving but he was drowning, and by the time he noticed what was happening, it was too late.

The same process would apply to the non-legal issues with him and his supporters. Here the lying, insulting, and threatening would have to be stopped. It would be achieved through a similar approach. He would have to get a taste of his own medicine. He liked to dish it out but could he take it? I doubted it.

A small group of twisted individuals, some thugs, and some paedophile enablers had to be challenged and dissuaded. One by one as they fell away or became effectively impotent, Bailey would become isolated; no longer would he have the 'adoration' of a few cheerleaders. He would be on his own and he would struggle to cope. He appeared to be weaker and more regularly drunk or stoned.

Bits by bit, cut by cut, he was deteriorating. The pressure being exerted on him was being cranked up. All the time it was important to focus on the truth, not lie like Bailey and his chums. As the pressure grew and the 'psychological energy ' needed to keep his head above water increased. His behaviour changed. Given he was so often drunk it is possible that Bailey did not even notice his struggle and loss of powers.

Whether he was conscious of it or it was an unconscious reaction he flailed around, spitting invective often completely incoherent, he was prone to childish tantrums. His low-grade infantile sense of humour was on show, It was not a good look. His limited energy was being sapped and not replaced.

He could dish it out but he could not take it

As Bailey liked to deal in petty insults he would be given a dose of his own medicine. To be fair he was often given many doses of his own medicine by many people, most days. He could not take it. He was not quick-witted and his sense of humour was severely limited. His standard comebacks amounted to calling people turds, langers, or masturbators. The lameness of his replies made the whole thing funnier and him look ever more absurd. At one time he could use an insult like turd or gobshite and his supporters would obediently laugh. With time all that changed. As his support dried up he looked ever more ridiculous.

How Ian Bailey learned to swim

With that in mind, I decided that one of the ways of irritating Bailey. Of getting at him. Would be to mock him. It was not something he had experienced in life. He expected people to defer to him for his looks his intelligence and his wit. So, it became my intention to mock him. I did this in many ways some of them quite subtle some of them rather less so. For example, he had been a bed wetter. He wet the bed well into his teens according to Elio Malocco in his book Killing Sophie. This is a serious medical condition. For many criminal psychologists, it is a red flag that children may have psychopathic tendencies. In most circumstances, this would not be an issue to be mocked. But this was Bailey and he needed to be taken down a peg or two.

This led me to use forms of childish teasing and taunting of Bailey that I was convinced would perturb him. I pondered aloud about him wetting his bed as a teenage boy which he certainly did. I suggested that it was so bad that he was able to learn the backstroke while lying in bed at night, that his sheets were sodden each morning. I should add here that one of the other revelations of the Malocco book stated that Bailey was a prodigious masturbator and that he started his interest in masturbation while looking at porn at the age of 12. This is an unnaturally early age to start. I almost shed a tear for his poor mother Brenda Bailey, each morning going into his bedroom wondering whether the sheets had been soiled with urine or semen. It was a game of bed-soiling roulette. One could not help feeling sorry for his parents.

Years of dealing with this 'cuckoo in the nest', and a urine-sodden cuckoo at that.

People started posting photographs of incontinence pads or man nappies to mock him. I also posited the possibility that every night when he went to bed in Glengariff or Bantry the sirens would start up warning locals there was a flooding threat in the area. I raised the possibility that he would be supplied with those sandbags that people are given to protect their homes at times of flooding. But in Bailey's case the sandbags would not be outside the house stopping the water from coming in they were inside his residence stopping his urine leaking out.

Not very funny? Rather low rent? I know, but still, it irked him and reminded people that he was far from perfect and he was perhaps better mocked than feared. It is difficult to fear a man squelching his way down the street. Psychologists call this reframing. He did not seem at all keen on being teased in this way. Good!

It was encouraging to note that as I started to tease him others joined in. Usually with far more wit and talent than I did. It became a communal effort, something that many of us enjoyed doing. While he hated it. Win- win. There would be regular tweets about him requiring man nappies or that he had not put on his man nappies that day. This would make the arrogant man a bit more self-conscious.

Teeth

One of the funniest and most telling sets of insults aimed at Bailey came when there was a photograph of him smiling into the camera. I say smile but it was probably a rictus grin. He was wearing dentures and the dentures were not clean, his teeth were filthy.

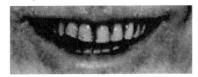

It was as if he could not be bothered to take them out at night and pop them in a glass with some cleaning formula. There was a rash of tweets about dentures and cleaning them. There were photographs of those wind-up teeth you can get that bounce around and chatter.

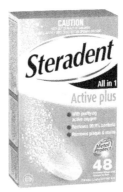

The comments and jokes did have an impact on Bailey. Within a few months, his dentures were decidedly cleaner. This must have been a major task. It was akin to cleaning off the bottom of an old oil tanker. One where all types of chemicals and machinery are needed to remove the barnacles stuck to the bottom. A few people have, on occasion, questioned my treatment of him. To them, I say this: "I significantly improved his oral hygiene, what did you ever do for him?"

This was not sophisticated humour. However, what it did was undermine the man. Narcissists want adoration, not contempt. To be revered not mocked. Things were shifting slowly.

Pin up

Despite him being comparatively young in his early 60's. People would joke about Bailey needing a Zimmer frame or shuffling along the streets wherever it was he lived.

He always considered himself a good catch. He thought he was a particularly good-looking man. Yet I met very few women who even when they've seen a photograph of him in his prime believed he was 'all that.' Whatever he was in the past by the time I got to see him and got to know him he was a wreck. He had that strange combination whereby some parts of his body. mainly around his gut and his man breasts, were overweight. Whereas other parts of his body appeared withered like he had lost a lot of muscle mass. I had no idea of his health conditions and I'm not an expert on them now but it has always looked as though he lived a very unhealthy lifestyle. People started taking photographs of him and posting them, showing his physical decline.

He admitted he was a very heavy drinker. In September and October 2023, Bailey was alleged to have had three heart attacks. The medical experts were unable to do extensive surgery on his heart due to underlying health conditions. This physical decline appears to have been accelerated when his long-term partner, Jules Thomas, kicked him out of her home. After decades of not holding down a full-time job and pottering around the Thomas properties, he was forced to leave by her and her daughters. It appeared that for a long time, he had failed to take the hint. Jules Thomas wanted him out. His many years of being subsidised by Thomas had ended. Bailey no longer had a free roof over his head, no warm bed, and no one buying his food, drink, and clothes for him. In his early 60's Ian needed to pull on his big boy pants and venture out into the world. It proved to be a bridge too far.

In no time at all it appeared that he was not eating healthily though managing to still consume a fair amount of alcohol. His appearance became increasingly shabby, the new clothes bought for him by Thomas would not be taken care of in the way they would have been had he still been living with her. We must remember here that he was living a subsidised life with Thomas for all the decades he was with her.

In all that time he had never been able to hold down a proper job. A job where he would turn up put in a shift and then go home. He seemed to think loafing around a few markets over the weekend flogging pizzas, plants, and bits of wood he played with during the week was in some way a career. It wasn't. He was in decline and it showed. He often needed sticks to walk. He shuffled around the streets. He looked incapable of running even a few yards. Despite all this, this gaunt feeble partially fat, partially skinny man with poor teeth, dreadful skin, and a poor sense of personal hygiene found plenty of time to insult other people on their appearance.

For Bailey, insulting people on the grounds of their physical appearance, their clothing, their alleged intelligence or status was common. What started to happen in 2021/22 was people started to hit back. The first factor driving this turnabout was his posting photographs of himself on social media. The boil-faced photograph and the image of his moob-revealing t-shirt were posted by Bailey. How could a man who looked like this dare to criticise others? The second factor was other people started to take photographs of Bailey in Glengarriff and Bantry. They captured the rapid decline in his condition. People could see how ridiculous it was that he was being rude to others. The worm had turned.

No one could be in any doubt that Bailey was a physical wreck, his clothes were scruffy and his hygiene lamentable. He was being called out by many people. They would laugh at his hypocrisy and point out his failings. A significant source of his personal power had been more than neutralised. It had been turned upon him.

Everyone knew it, including Bailey.

Images of Bailey posted by him and others turned the tables on his personal insults

Fully ulcerated legs

Boil covered face

The Bailey t-shirt shows his moobs and beer gut

Selling books at the edge of Bantry market

Pushing an empty trolley

Filthy bandaged feet

I was described as being short and fat and tramp-like. I'm no oil painting don't get me wrong. But I'm almost 6 foot one, I'm not fat and I consider myself to have a reasonable build. I'm not scruffy and I have decent personal hygiene but that's not the way he chose to see it. He's also called women who dare to disagree with him short and fat and ugly. It is pathetic. It is what silly little schoolboys do or emotionally inadequate adults. So, I guess perhaps it's not too surprising that he resorted to those insults. Once he was on the receiving end of a few mild insults he struggled. This is typical of bullies. he really could not hack it.

The Glengarriff Incident April 2022

In early April I travelled down to Glengarriff. I took a walk around the Bamboo Park and had some lunch. I knew Bailey lived in the Glen as he was forever referring to his accommodation at Perrins Inn. He had moved there temporarily after his partner removed him from her home.

I drove into the town to source a hotel venue for an event where there would be readings from chapter eight of Elio Malocco's book, Killing Sophie. That was the chapter based on Bailey's journals and diaries. It spelled out his long-term interest in hardcore pornography, masturbation, rigorous anal sex, and a sexual interest in underage girls.

I parked up at Quills wool store and my wife walked towards the entrance. She returned immediately saying that Bailey was seated outside Perrins, alone and playing with his mobile phone. He appeared to have aged considerably since the last time I saw him. I had no idea that he would be there that day. He could have been out and about in West Cork, perhaps at court, frequenting bars, or hiding in his room. Yet later his narcissism and paranoia would cause him to assume my presence there that day was part of some cunning plan to ambush him.

After visiting a few places along the main road, I found an excellent venue. The hotel day manager was married to an ex-UK Police officer who had been involved in a major police project that one of my family members had been part of. She knew who Bailey was. I walked back towards where I was parked. I saw that he was still sitting there. I stopped and said hello. I was standing approximately five metres away from him on a sunny spring afternoon. This detail is significant for much of what follows. I told him that I had been talking about him. That got his interest and he put down his phone. When I mentioned the Malocco readings he grimaced and chuntered. I told him I would see him around and crossed the road to Quills. The whole exchange took less than a minute. I was surprised at how irritated he was but thought little of it.

Over the next few days, I mentioned the brief meeting to a few people. However, he was working himself up into a very emotional state. The man who wanted always to control the agenda had been pushed onto the back foot. My presence and the reason I was there had rattled him. I had inadvertently parked my tank on his lawn. Within a few days, I would learn just how bitter and twisted he was.

Bailey tended to tweet very infrequently but on April 7th he became far more active.

Ian Kenneth Bailey BCL, LLB, LLM (UCC)

@IanKennethBail1

A funny thing happened earlier this week…I was writing outside in the village where I live and an old tramp came up and said he was planning to do a reading about me Good luck I told him. Afterwards I checked the CCTV and I think he is a well known criminal psychopath. More t f

1.51PM-Apr 7, 2022

Ian Kenneth Bailey BCL, LLB, LLM (UCC)

@IanKennethBail1

Oh really…I had a funny thought it might be a troll… If it was him his demeanor might explain a lot… This character was dirty, very small and quite ugly with weird eyes

7.52PM – Apr 7, 2022

Ian Kenneth Bailey BCL, LLB, LLM (UCC)

@IanKennethBail1

The CCTV picked up clear image which I have screen shot… Thank you for that

7.54PM – Apr 7, 2022

Ian Kenneth Bailey BCL, LLB, LLM (UCC)

@IanKennethBail1

Hello friends, fans , followers, and the very trolls. It is my suspicion that the Arch troll JP Areseholzer is on the loose in Ireland… He is clearly a dangerous lunatic so if anyone wants to go after him and challenge him to reveal his true identity I will meet him and teach him

8.04PM – Apr 7, 2022

On April 7th Bailey started having a meltdown that reverberated to the day he died. No one had ever seen him this het up on social media. He had lost the initiative; he had lost control. From that day onwards he was on the back foot and he never recovered control.

He said I was a dangerous lunatic, one of many labels he would slap on me in the years to come, with no effect. He asked his 5000+ followers to accost me in the street and demand that I identify myself. This is an obsession that never ended. The ace investigative newshound never discovered who I was to his last day. His followers, many fake, would struggle to find me. His description of me was totally inaccurate. Furthermore, I have several distinguishing features that went unmentioned. Whoever he was describing in his tweets it was not me! He had no observational skills at all, the man was delusional. Could it have been alcohol, drugs, or rank stupidity that caused this? Probably all three.

This is how I immediately knew Bailey did not have any CCTV of me. He could not have photographic images of me and get it so wrong. He was lying to everyone. He was trying to get me to stand down with this ploy. I wondered how many times he had lied about having information that could damage people and bullied them into submission. But not this time. From this point on I knew he was a third-rate bully with a limited repertoire built mainly on extravagant lies.

When he said he would meet me and teach me I suggested the Skibbereen market the following Saturday, April 9th. I was there. He hid in his Glengarriff gaff. Drunk and angry and hiding in his room. His threat that I would meet my demise was an empty one. His cowardice was now a matter of record. Many people could see he had a big mouth and no balls.

He knew deep down he had been humiliated and he became increasingly reckless. No doubt fuelled by cheap alcohol. I had not humiliated him per se. He had done that to himself by being trapped in his lies and empty threats.

Bailey became desperate. His behaviour had become fevered. A brief conversation with a stranger in Glengarriff had led to him becoming very angry and agitated. He was asking everyone and anyone to identify me. He posted his email address and phone number asking people to give him my private details. His social media output about me was repeatedly foul and vulgar. He asked his followers to accost me in the street and he threatened me with violence. In many ways, he never threw off of that anger.

This response was over the top. Completely out of proportion compared with the event that caused it. Going from a conversation about a reading event to threats of meeting and teaching, and a person's demise. This was demented. If he could become so aggressive and unstable over a book reading what might he be like if a partner opposed him behind closed doors, or a woman, alone in the middle of the night, turned down his sexual advances? I think we all know.

The doxing begins Mid-April 2022

As I mocked him for chickening out of a face-to-face meeting his temperament reached fever pitch. I had also picked out one of his newspaper features and dismantled it.(Appendix2) This was another thing Bailey had not experienced and he did not like it. He became obsessed with finding out who I was. He was asking, even begging, people to tell him who I was and where I lived. He would not address the issues, instead, he sought to bully the questioner. Sound familiar?

This led to an episode that was both hilarious, in demonstrating the hatred-fueled nature of Bailey and his crew and damning in the way he and others wrongly and callously named an innocent party in their haste to hurt me.

In essence, he claimed to have a top team of technology geniuses who could name me and dox me. He often referred to having such teams of people. It was a source of great merriment to many of us: 'There he goes again; he has another elite team working for him.' These people were never named nor did they go public on who they were. Most likely they were a small number of supporters fuelled by their petty grudges.

This led to an extremely funny outcome after his 'experts' decided that I was a Dublin-based businessman. They got photographs of that man and then (I am laughing here) checked it was the correct man by asking Bailey to ID the man he saw in Glengarriff. He said yes and they believed him! How could anyone believe Bailey? They could not have asked to see his CCTV images. If they asked and he told them he had lied about the CCTV they should have walked away. When he had no CCTV images were they not suspicious? Evidently not.

Bailey's elite/crack teams

A group of unknown and unnamed experts in their field, For reasons never explained they are happy to work for a penniless tramp with no manners or discernible talent.

They were so desperate to get the businessman that they all confirmed each other's blind prejudices. What a sad bunch. Sadly, they wrongly named a man. They posted several photographs of him, and published details about his professional and private life. They were lucky that the victim did not press charges and or sue them. With Bailey now dead and his electronic devices in the hands of the Police, these bullying experts may soon be named.

It was at this time that the victim of this incompetent doxing asked me to make it clear that the Holzer account was not run by him. I was happy to do so. This meant that by the end of April 2022, AGS knew who I was, unequivocally.

I mention this because poor sad Ian was to try and intimidate me throughout 2023 by claiming he had reported me for a hate crime in the UK. It had been reported to an unspecified police force at an unspecified time with unspecified and allegations. He made it known that the UK police force would only act when they received a submission from AGS. The submission would be sent to the UK once AGS had my details. Once again, I knew the old fool was lying. AGS had all of my details. They had them a year earlier. His story was a complete fabrication. The man was desperate.

In an earlier attempt to intimidate me, he claimed he submitted complaints about me to the Yorkshire and Lancashire police force. What was the nature of his complaint? That a man with a Twitter account who he could not name and did not know where exactly he lived was being nasty to him. What made this bunch of lies funnier was that Yorkshire and Lancashire had, between them, 7 separate forces. I think it safe to conclude he did not contact any of them. They never contacted me. These were the idle threats of a loser and it showed.

Bailey, not a man able to learn from his many failures, went on to try and dox me several times more. Occasionally he merely labeled me a criminal psychopath, a psychiatric patient, or a prisoner. He went a little further a few weeks after the failed Dublin man effort. He then claimed I was a corrupt ex-UK copper who had been kicked out of the force. Once again it was nonsense. I was made aware that this information was being fed to Bailey by someone who hated him. A long list of such people existed. He was so full of hate that he did not attempt to check this story. He got it gloriously wrong, again. He made a complete ass of himself, again. He had gone from puppet master to headless chicken in a matter of weeks.

By now the stress on Bailey was considerable. He would be increasingly anxious and tired. He would be inclined to up his level of self-medication with alcohol, Over a sustained period he would manifest psychological and physical decline would accelerate.

I should mention that later he claimed to have outed me a third time. That time he clutched some comments by a follower, obviously did no checks, and announced that I live in Sheffield and had convictions for domestic violence. Wrong! His failure amused me and others while eating away at him. Win-Win.

Ian runs to Mummy Bracken at the newspaper

At this time, before the first foul doxing was proven to be a tissue of lies, in typical Bailey fashion, he ran to the newspapers with a silly story. Not for the first or last time would his falsehoods be presented as facts. He told the journalist a series of lies. However, he had got it wrong. Completely wrong. The man looked nothing like me, I had never worked nor lived in Dublin. There was no stalking. He was neither scared nor uneasy.

	Independent on Sunday May 1st, 2022
Ian Bailey 'targeted in person by web troll' ALI BRACKEN Ian Bailey has complained to gardaí after coming face-to-face with an online troll who tracked him down in West Cork.	"He then told me he would see me at Skibbereen market. I have gone to gardaí. I have established this individual's identity. He lives in Dublin. So he travelled a long way to see me.

On May 7th Bailey was forced to make a typical, faux, apology.

Ian Kenneth Bailey BCL,LLB,LLM (UCC)

@IanKennethBail1

So I am informed I was recently set up by a small number of Twitter users and was mislead about certain information and it appears it may not have been a small man called James Galvin and if such a person exist I apologies for any confusion…we are all human and sometimes er…

2.24pm 7 May 2022

He knew the man he had doxed existed and he got it wrong. He would have only made such an apology under some form of duress. He lacked the balls to openly admit he was wrong and so reluctantly produced these weasel words.

While they were disingenuous they still gave me considerable pleasure. He would hate making any apology. Somewhere in his psyche, he would know he was losing the battle. His best efforts were no good and he was being pressured. This would strain him even more. On days when there were no interactions between him and his foes this new reality of failure and not controlling the narrative would each at him.

His use of the press was a common theme. It was no longer working. The most disappointing aspect of these events was that journalists did not follow up on most of these stories. They did not fact checking and they did not hold him to account. He used them to get at other people. Some journalists were being manipulated by a lying drunk.

He was to go to the press many times with tales aimed at intimidating others. Sometimes he would combine a press story with one of his other favourite attack lines. He loved to threaten people that he was making formal complaints to AGS. He would do so while at the same time mentioning that he had three law degrees. In doing so he wanted the person(s) being threatened to believe that his legal qualification meant his complaint was credible. The complaint he made to AGS on May 29th, 2022, was publicised by social media and mainstream media.

Call the Cops: Using AGS to try and intimidate people

Bailey had been flattened by the events of April and May 2022. The challenges to him were starting to bite extremely hard. He was putting a huge amount of effort in and being routinely humiliated.

Bailey posted a complaint on Twitter that he submitted to officers at Bantry barracks. That is exactly what he handed in. We shouldn't forget that this was handed in by a man who boasts of having three law degrees. He says he is a legal academic – whatever that is – yet he produced this strange document. It is creased, wrinkled, and has several smudges. The thought of him shuffling up to Bantry station and handing over that piece of paper was very entertaining. Had he submitted his complaint on toilet paper written in crayon, it would not have been less impressive than the smudged note. The 'big tough guy' thought this would deter us. This was all he had left in his locker. He should have left it there. He was finished.

In the complaint, he childishly refers to himself as a 'social media virgin.' He refers to nasty, malicious, and factually flawed claims against him. He fails to name one solitary example. Nor did he ever provide any evidence. This is Bailey telling lies and creating fiction in an attempt to intimidate people who challenged him. This is less a one-off occurrence and more a lifestyle choice. With the three people named this was not going to work. He expected people to back off when he stuck the boot in. He was perplexed when this did not happen.

May 29th, 2022

Statement from Ian K. Bailey, BC.L. LLLM made on May 26th at Bantry Garda Station.

I make this statement knowing if any of the information is false I am likely to face prosecution.

In June of 2021 I lost my Social Media virginity and opened accounts on Facebook, Instagram and Twitter. I immediately became aware on Twitter that there were a number of anonymous accounts engaged in an apparently orchestrated "trolling" campaign and they publishing nasty, malicious and factually flawed claims against me. This persisted throughout 2021 and into 2022 [Although they seem to have quietened down a fair bit].

There were 3 accounts that stood out 1. JPHOLZER2021@JHolzer2021 2. COUNTESS BOUVIER@COUNTESSBOUVIER and 3. FETH FIADH@BERNADE88965032.

JPHOLZER would appear to live in Leeds, Yorkshire. On April 7th last at 12.30 I was sat outside the Perria Inn, Glengarriff, when I was approached by a man who said he was looking for a venue to read extracts from a book by a defrocked solicitor David Elio Malocco. The following Saturday I saw the same man at Skibbereen Market. I did not engage with him.

I believe this man is behind the account JPHOLZER as he subsequently tweeted he had encountered me in Glengarriff. I found the whole episode sinister and worrying.

Regarding the other 2 FETH FIADH is a ____ shopkeeper called ____ and COUNTESS BOUVIER would appear to be living in the Schull, Ballydehob, Bantry area.

Tiss my belief that 3 of these shadow characters has broken the law and I would ask AGS to investigate this worrying matter.

He did see me in Glengarriff but did not see me the following Saturday. He did not turn up. He preferred to hide in his room in Glengarriff. In the complaint, he claimed that the event was sinister and worrying, yet in his tweets at the time he said something completely different. That is 100% Bailey, he struggled to keep his story straight never mind true. He got names wrong and guessed where people lived. It is a shambles. He finishes his complaint by using the rarely used legal phrase ' tiss my belief.' The evidence-free, kvetching of a man with a sloppy mind and too much time on his hands. This was one of his last throws of the dice and it flopped. Ultimately AGS could not investigate the case because he could provide no substance. The hollow moaning in the written complaint was all he could muster. That was all he had. To summarise, Bailey was saying he could not cope with being challenged. Boo hoo. It was not going to get any better for him.

If he had pressed harder there is every chance AGS would have asked to see his phone and computer. That was never going to happen. Too many dark secrets. Now he is dead we may learn of what secrets they held.

Getting to know each other

Bailey became obsessed with me. He was irritated by what I said, so I was quickly making progress. This has led to him telling people he ignored me while in truth he was desperate to find out who I was, until the day he died. He had asked many people, those he knew and strangers to discover my identity. I had become an itch he could not scratch. He made a fool of himself by incorrectly doxing me not once but three times! Each time his desperation has resulted in him naming people who are nothing like me.

The man who talked up his newspaper credentials, who bragged of being an investigative journalist for the Sunday Times did not appear to use several unimpeachable sources to reach his conclusions. He was a man who made it up or who grasped at any rumour from any single source if what he heard would confirm his maniacal prejudices.

By the autumn of 2022, Bailey had very few active supporters. People online and off no longer feared him. He was shifting from someone feared and in control to someone who was laughed at in the streets and no longer in charge of events. Online, people laughed off his best attempts to denigrate them. He had to try harder but could make no progress. More and more energy was expelled for lesser and lesser effect. To do so is stressful and tiring. When the main method for ameliorating the stress was cheap alcohol, the long-term prognosis was not good.

Anal Ian

Ian had an anal issue. A trip through his social media output leaves us in no doubt. Much of this was aimed at me but not exclusively. Bailey would invariably call me Arseholzer or Arseholer. It seemed to give him a lot of pleasure. He did not stop there. He loved words like turd, gobshyte, and excrement. He would use them repeatedly. Often trying to cram all of them into a single tweet or message. He succeeded in doing so many times. This task was made easier because he had long since given up any pretence of being coherent.

He was fixated on anal words. We know from his diaries that he was also obsessed with anal sex. I hope you are not eating as you read this. Freudians would have a field day with his interests. What on earth happened during Ian's potty training? The mind boggles. I feel for his parents. Imagine having to bring up this strange creature.

The attempted assassination of Ian Bailey (allegedly)

To be fair there was no assassination attempt, you knew that. Instead, we have him doing the same old stuff. Lying, insulting, and running to the press. He was such a wuss.

Trying to make a mountain out of a molehill and failing. This is how it panned out.

On July 10th, 2022, Jon Kierans reported in the Irish Mirror

Ian Bailey confronted and abused by two angry women who shouted 'murderer, murderer' as the manned market stall (Excerpts)

Ian Bailey was confronted and abused by two angry women about the unsolved killing of French woman Sophie Toscan du Plantier over the weekend.

They publicly shouted "murderer, murderer" at him as he manned a market stall in Bantry, Co Cork on Friday in front of hundreds of people.

They then turned up to a local bar the following evening, where Mr Bailey was reading poetry at the West Cork Literary Festival.

They once again started heckling him and were eventually asked to leave by the manager and security staff.

Bailey did not have a stall in the actual market. To do so would require the payment of a fee. The money from these fees helped pay for the market and its promotion. Furthermore, to have a stall required that he possessed the appropriate insurance. He was a lifelong scrounger. He wanted to benefit from the market day but put nothing in. He preferred to piggyback on hard-working people. It was forever thus.

The Kierans article appeared straightforward. Honest peace-loving Ian Bailey was set upon by two angry shouting and screaming women in Bantry market and then later at the Maritime Hotel. You might also believe that Bailey was having his poetry event at the hotel. The article stated, as a fact, that the manager and security staff asked the women to leave. But wait, let's see another report.

July 10th, 2022, Neesa Cumiskey reported in the Sunday World

FAT CHANCE | Ian Bailey claims 'two fat ladies' heckled him at poetry reading

(Excerpts)

Ian Bailey has claimed that that he was "heckled" by "two fat ladies" at a Cork literary festival over the weekend.

The festival hosted an open mic opportunity for attendees to recite poetry or tell stories.

Bailey claims that he was taunted by the women while he was onstage and said that the pair were escorted out of the venue by hotel security.

"there was poetry and storytelling... only spoiled for a moment by two fat ladies who heckled me a bit before being ejected by hotel security..".

However, neither the hotel hosting the event nor the organisers of the West Cork Literary Festival could confirm that Bailey was heckled.

A spokesperson for the festival said that they have not been made aware of any disruptions during yesterday's event.

She added that while Bailey does "live locally", he was not specifically invited to attend the festival.

But the open mic is all welcome. We have no control of who attends. It basically gives the opportunity to anyone to attend and they get about 3 or 4 minutes to speak their poetry or readings. But they're not specifically invited to attend."

In this second version, his claims are put into inverted commas. These are things said by Bailey but unverified. Once again he feels compelled to offer childish insults. His descriptions of the women were factually untrue. Just the low rent jibes of a man perturbed by two women who would not be cowed by him. The article checks the facts and discovers neither the hotel nor the Festival organisers reported any disturbances or ejections by security staff. He was lying. It is a shame the first article relied solely on the copy provided by Bailey.

The truth is that in the marketplace there were not two angry women shouting murderer at the tops of their voices. But two women who were willing to stand up to Bailey. When one of the women explained that she was the woman who had called him out over the grooming, He was visibly shaken. It was he who became aggressive. When the woman suggested they both go to the Police station and make formal complaints about each other it was him who snarled 'F*** Off' and then beat a hasty retreat. Well, as hasty as a man in his condition could muster.

The open-night poetry event was just as it had been described by the Festival spokesperson. It was not Bailey's gig. Like the others there, he had a few minutes to read a couple of poems. If people were to heckle, that would be no surprise. That is what happens at open mic events. In reality, he had been spooked by the presence of the women. They had the temerity to go 'toe to toe' with him and he bottled it. The truth was that as soon as he waffled through his manky poems he sat on one of the front seats staring straight ahead, not daring to turn around for a few recitals. Then seeing the women had left he got up and made a beeline for the exit.

The 'short fat' man in Glengarriff had been joined by two other 'short fat people.' And this time they were women! Yes, women. He was learning the hard way that people were not going to be intimidated by him. Worse still, for him, one of the women from Co Mayo was the person Bailey had sought to bully and threaten when she called out his grooming.

She had got under the pervert's skin. When challenged by a determined woman a new pattern of behaviour by Bailey emerged. On Twitter, he retreated and blocked, in the market he had turned on his heels and fled, and in the hotel, he ran for the exit. For the next eighteen months, Bailey's frequent social media outbursts would often include invective aimed at that woman. She was an itch he could not scratch and he hated it 🫖

The cumulative effect of all these challenges to him, and a refusal to be bullied by him, was to stress him. He was no longer controlling his social media environment and he hated it. His repertoire of control techniques was not working. That is an extremely uncomfortable place to be for a narcissist. These were the signs of the behemoth cracking. It was delicious that he and his couple of close cultists could not see it. Furthermore at least part of his psyche would recognise that he was being pushed against his will. And that recognition would stress him further. See how it works? Bailey didn't. Things were going to get even worse for this 'playground bully'. He was finished, but this was only the beginning.

CHAPTER 5

Bailey is a Barefaced Liar

Pathological liar:

A pathological liar is an individual who chronically tells grandiose lies that may stretch or exceed the limits of believability. While most people lie or at least bend the truth occasionally, pathological liars do so habitually.

"I would copper bottom anything that I was going to say was fact."

Ian Bailey on The Shattered Lives podcast 13.03.2023

[He was lying]

For centuries it was easier for the pathological liar to get away with it. They would lie and then move on to their next lie. Their lies were not recorded or traceable. With the new communications technologies including social media, it is far more difficult to get away with lying. Ian Bailey grew up in the lower technology world where old-style lying could go unchallenged but things became different.

For example, on the Nial Boylan radio show, in the summer of 2021, on the subject of whether he ever met Sophie, He wanted his version of events to be believed rather than that of Sophie's neighbour Alfie Lyons. So, he claimed that he has an eidetic – photographic – memory. Implying his version of events must be true. However, when interviewed by the Sun newspaper, in January 2022, and asked about his implicating statements made soon after Sophie's death, he claimed the lies and falsehoods were attributable to memory failures. The observable reality is that he did not have a perfect memory nor was he cognitively impaired in 1996. He would say whatever he thought would make him look good in the moment. Always a case of narcissistic expediency over the truth.

We know that at the time of the murder and afterward he repeatedly lied. Sometimes giving four or five contradictory versions of the same events. He speaks, he lies. He told many lies to AGS about what he did on the night of the 21st of December. He lied about where he was on the evening of the 22nd, and lied about the route home and whether he stopped or not on the way home. Most significantly he gave AGS a false alibi for where he was when Sophie was murdered. A false alibi that was originally endorsed by Jules Thomas. He has made at least 50 substantial changes in his statements about the murder. This was not just lying; this was Ian Bailey lying.

Ian Bailey is a liar. He lies regularly and he lies about things small and large. When you take a close look at all these lies it becomes impossible to trust anything he might say on any subject. Anyone hearing statements by him is well advised to look for verification of what he says. His word counts for nothing. If he cannot provide cast iron proof the best bet is to treat what he says as the self-serving opinion of a lying drunk rather than fact.

In the week commencing October 9th, 2023, Bailey was residing at Bantry Hospital. Earlier he claimed to have had his third heart attack in a month. We know this because he was able to give an interview to journalist John Kierans from his 'death bed'. Strangely, fearing he was about to die in his flat he put on his hat and coat, left his flat, and locked the door. Strolled down to his car and drove himself to the hospital. A very strange response to a heart attack. Most people ring for an ambulance.

During his hospital stay, he gave an interview to PJ Coogan on the Cork 96fm radio station. As is his wont Bailey wanted to read his risible poetry on air. He claimed it was a new poem inspired by the wonderful nurses and staff at the hospital. The poem, called Superglue, was typically a childish doggerel. It was not the content that piqued my interest. Instead, I was reminded how effortlessly and regularly he lied to people.

The poem spoken by him in October 2023 is available on his TIKTOK account. He read it out on March 2nd, 2023, it was titled 'Handy'. By the time he read it to PJ Coogan, it was at least 7 months old and decidedly not written for the nurses tending to him. His contempt for Mr Coogan, the nurses, and the listeners could not be more evident. As we will see nor was this the first time that he lied about his poetry.

The types of lies told by Bailey

As the lies are numerous and varied it will be helpful to put the man's lies into several categories. Sometimes a lie will apply to more than one category.

Self-Aggrandisement – As a narcissist Bailey had a very high opinion of himself. His problem was that he achieved so little. Much has been abject failure resulting in him being unable to support himself and being dependent on the state. This has resulted in many lies that attempt to bolster his limited achievements.

Denigrating others – An offshoot from the lies to 'big himself up' are the lies he tells to 'talk other people down'. These are often people who challenge him. People whom he is incapable of taking on in argument. Instead, he calls them revolting childish names, plus he lies about them, to try and denigrate them.

Truth avoidance and covering other lies – there are a raft of lies that he tells to hide the truth. Often these are lies that show him to be far from the 'successful person' he says he is. More interestingly he has lied about the Sophie Toscan du Plantier murder. For decades he has lied to hide information about this case.

Situational lies – this is a catch-all type of lying that is deployed by repeat liars. When in a certain situation he lied as a means to wriggle out of an immediate problem.

Victim narratives – A recent and growing development in his range of lies has been his reliance on playing the victim.

Self- Aggrandisement

The example told to Cork 96 FM when Bailey claimed he has almost spontaneously penned a poem inspired by the nurses is an example of the man trying to look gifted and caring. It is him saying look at me aren't I something. Once the truth is known it says look at me I am inadequate, I will lie about irrelevant items to boost my flaccid self- image. Similarly, on August 19th, 2023, he posted another poem on TIKTOK bragging it was new. However, 13 months earlier he read the same poem on a Dynamo Kelly podcast. These examples are not slips or errors they were his daily routines. Many of his lies and falsehoods focused on talking him up.

There is more, much more. For his 'In My Own Words podcast,' he promised 6 x 2-hour episodes beginning in September or October 2022. He delivered just 3 episodes which offered less than 2 hours of content in total. The first was not released until April 2023. He repeatedly changed the number of episodes, what would be in each of them, and the release dates. He said he would do an episode answering listeners' questions he did not do so. He also ducked away from answering questions about the podcast when repeatedly questioned by people on social media. Often he blocked people asking legitimate questions. Strictly speaking these are not lies. They do show a man who makes aggrandising promises who cannot deliver. A man whose word means nothing. He is all talk but completely unreliable. This will be explored in more detail in chapters 6, 7 and 8.

He has promised a concert tour with his perfected 2-hour show. Nothing happened. He claimed he had a huge backlog of shoutout requests for TIKTOK and then there were only a couple of them. A repeated theme, big talk often covered by lazy or gullible journalists and then nothing. The sad part here is not a single journalist has followed up his empty assertions and called him out on them. Not one. This way of operating showed us a man relying on off-the-cuff falsehoods over hard work and substantive results.

The self-aggrandising lies about podcast downloads

Returning to the calamitous Bailey podcast. He had spent months claiming it would be his legacy (it was, but not the way he hoped). Once the episodes were launched the real public response was anything from indifference through to derision. So, we then got some lies. He claimed well over 20,000 downloads of his 3 recordings. He boasted of being a podcast sensation. Only his words. No proof was ever provided. It could not be, it did not exist.

Ian Kenneth Bailey BCL, LLB, LLM (UCC) @IanKennethBail1 · Jun 10   ···
So Friends, Fans, Followers and Foolish Fouls...Episode 2 of my Podcast
IAN BAILEY IN HIS OWN WORDS...FROM PARADISE FOUND TO PARADISE
LOST...Will be available free next week...Thank you to the 10,000 plus
listeners and all the positive complimentary feedback 😊 😊 😊

Ian Kenneth Bailey BCL, LLB, LLM (UCC) @IanKennethBail1 · Jun 14 ···
So FFF and The Odd Foul 😃 😃 😃 The 2nd Chapter of my Podcast...IAN
BAILEY IN HIS OWN WORDS...Has been downloaded almost 20 000
times...Thank Ye

   ◯ 1   ↻ 1   ♡ 4   ılı 3,266   ↑

↻ Ian Kenneth Bailey BCL, LLB, LLM (UCC) reposted

Ian Kenneth Bailey BCL, LLB, LLM (UCC) @IanKennethBail1 · Jun 13 ···
So FFFs and Few Fouls...Thank ye so much for positive feedback on my first
Pod Carst...IAN BAILEY IN HIS OWN WORDS...My techies tell me close to
20,000 down loads in 1st 72 hours...If u liked/enjoyed Ep 2...Wait until ye
ear Ep3.Slan 😃 😃 😃

   ◯ 2   ↻ 1   ♡ 9   ılı 4,134   ↑

   ◯   ↻   ♡   ılı 1,608   ↑

Ian Kenneth Bailey BCL, LLB, LLM (UCC) @IanKennethBail1 · Jun 16 ···
Thank you to one my 5000 FB folllowers for pointing out typographical
error...earlier this my Podcast had received 2000 downloads not 20'000
😃 😃 😃

   ◯ 2   ↻   ♡ 2   ılı 2,296   ↑

Ian Kenneth Bailey BCL, LLB, LLM (UCC) @IanKennethBail1 · Jul 4 ···
So Friends, Fans, Followers and few remaining, cowardly, Hate Speech
Foolish Fouls...Hit 5000 plus Down Loads of 2nd Chapter of My
Podcarsrt...IB in his own Words and the 99.9 pc who have indicated
positive response...Wait till ye ear CHAPTER 3....Available Soon...Abu Abu
😃 😃 😃

   ◯ 4   ↻   ♡ 13   ılı 3,201   ↑

Bailey claims 5000+ downloads of episode 2 with 99.9%
positive responses. That means 4995 positive responses.
There was no evidence supporting any of this. He was

repeatedly asked to provide proof of the downloads and feedback at every turn. Evidence was kryptonite to Bailey.

Ian Kenneth Bailey BCL, LLB, LLM (UCC) @IanKennethBail1 · Aug 8   ···
SO IAN BAILEY IN HIS OWN WORDS PODCAST IN TOP 25 PERCENT OF
PODCASTS DOWNLOADED...IN EXCESS OF 15,000...

Yet despite being asked many times to prove it, a very easy thing to do, he refused and sometimes blocked the people asking for proof. He had once occupied a world where he could lie and move on. His lies were treated as facts. But this had changed. A growing group of people were civilly and persistently asking for answers and the pathological liar had none. He was finding it nearly impossible to face up to his deceptions. It was exhausting.

Where on earth could he find testable evidence that he had 4995 positive feedback? His lies had not only become excessive and unverifiable they had become preposterous. Every time he spewed forth another whopper, people just laughed.

He was learning that his empty lies were no longer good enough He claimed to have legions of people congratulating him on the podcasts. The pattern was clear big talk, but no evidence. He could not sustain a way of living he had enjoyed for over 50 years.

Other outrageous self-aggrandising claptrap

Bailey lies about birthday well-wishers

In 2023 it transpired that Bailey had got his date of birth wrong on his Facebook page. So starved of any support and interest was Bailey that when a few followers wished him happy birthday he did not correct the error preferring to hear a few kind words.

 My second arrest was on my birthdate 27.1.57...dont know why they got it wrong...had over 1,000 happy birthdays on FB

Not content with a couple of dozen people wishing him a happy birthday he felt compelled to make a ludicrous assertion. That he had over a thousand happy birthday greetings on Facebook. A quick check revealed that none of these were observable. They could have been by private messages but that was highly unlikely. The trackable nature of social media made it easy to expose his lies. His behaviour left a digital trail. A trail that showed him to be a dishonest man.

Entrepreneur hot shot

He claims to have sizable business deals and meetings with the high and mighty but nothing ever transpires. All these 'arrangements' always lack specifics such as names, dates, and details about the content of deals. This vagueness had two sources, First, they were fictional so there were no specifics. Second, by being vague Bailey ensured that none of his false claims could be disproven.

Eternal youth

He would claim he was youthful. This is despite the evidence provided by a quick look in the mirror. His filthy false teeth, his deformed feet, and his ulcerated legs were ignored. The bags under his eyes, his prominent moobs, and his atrocious skin were actively forgotten by the rapidly deteriorating man. A man who could hardly walk never mind run. He was in truth in an appalling state.

How young are ye...Im 66 yet still feeling 16

 Are ye on whatsupp

 Although I am now Vintage...peopele tell me I look 50s

Who were the people who told this man he looked to be in his 50s? there is little evidence that these people existed with the possible exception of sex workers/con artists happy to flatter a fool to get his money.

The drunken failure was randomly picking large numbers of well-wishers to try and bolster his popularity, claiming business success to elevate his status and claim to be youthful and attractive. It was pitiful. It was desperate. In private moments he must know he is lying. He increasingly knew he was not believed and was often mocked. He simply could not face up to reality. Time and again one asks why a man behaves this way. How vast must be his inner insecurity, his inner emptiness? From 2021 onwards he could no longer get away with this tired flim-flam.

His only way to feel less impotent and more than a failure was to come up with ever more ludicrous stories. But each time he did he was knocked down. Stressed and pummelled while being psychologically underdeveloped, his only response was to make even more outrageous claims. Each time the new ridiculous claim was stomped underfoot. It was a vicious spiral and he could not escape.

Denigrating others

When Bailey is challenged by people about his self-aggrandising lies, his failings, his crimes, and his perverse interest in underage girls he cannot argue his case as he has no facts and evidence. Instead of conceding his many failings or shutting up. He uses schoolboy insults and tells lies about his adversary.

I have personal experience of this. It showed me clearly that Bailey is intellectually limited, insecure, and a prolific liar. After I spoke to him briefly in Glengarriff, standing no

more than twenty feet away from him he went online with a
stream of lies. Evidently, the prospect of us making people
aware of his twisted sexual interests as described in Elio
Malocco's book: Killing Sophie, unnerved Bailey.

He said I was a short fat tramp, ugly with weird eyes, and
a known criminal psychopath.(all lies) He repeated these lies
more than once while leaving out things about my actual
appearance that any sane person would highlight. He said
I was a Dublin-based businessman and posted alleged photos
of me (lie and lie). He said I was a corrupt UK cop with the
initials J G and posted an alleged photo of me (lie, lie, and
lie). Later I was a resident of Sheffield with convictions for
domestic violence (lie and lie). He claimed he had CCTV
of me (lie), had photos of me more than once (lie) and I was
thrown out of a bar in Glengarriff (lie). Safe to say there is a
pattern here. He was totally out of control. And all because
I spoke to him for a few seconds.

We can see why the man who openly bragged about being
a Sunday Times journalist did not get a full-time. job there,

did not last very long and the examples of his work are rarer than hen's teeth. He would run to the press and lie to them as he did when claiming to be stalked in Glengarriff. The complaint to AGS about several people and then tweeting the complaint and getting stories in the newspapers all show Bailey energetically pushing lies.

His accusations that I was guilty of hate crimes is yet another example of the liar lying. He lied about his grooming behaviour and lied about a woman having convictions for prostitution and having press clippings to support it. He was a nonstop liar and with time people realised he was firing blanks.

Ian Kenneth Bailey BCL, LLB, LLM (U... @IanKennethB... · May 9, 2022 ···

So just for the odd anaraks out there...the throll Feth Fiadh (Who is none other than   of   had a very interesting alternative life style while living in Australia as a Working Girl...It's a most interesting and almost unbelievable sceal...TBC

His lies were everywhere and everywhere they were disproven. Other people on the receiving end of Bailey's denigrating lies include authors such as Elio Malocco, Nick Foster, and Michael Sheridan, several AGS officers including Dermot Dwyer, and Netflix. Recently he appeared to have turned on Jules Thomas and her daughters.

Each lie of this kind is an open message that he had no arguments, he was busted and somewhere deep inside him, he knew it.

Coda – as I started writing this book Ian Bailey posted this tweet

Ian Kenneth Bailey BCL, LLB, LLM (UCC)
@IanKennethBail1

So its interesting to note how spineless jellyfish accounts such as JPArseHolzer speil vile bile...The HAMAS defender and pro gender bender sits in the North of England pushing out hate speech and demonstrable nonsense presumably under influence of alcohol and God knows wat else

11:44 AM · Oct 17, 2023 · **674** Views

Bailey perfectly demonstrated a man with no coherent arguments and out of his depth. He spits out lies and little boy insults. More a tantrum than a tweet.

Truth avoidance and covering other lies

Perhaps the lies for which he is best known are those told to avoid the truth, particularly regarding the murder of Sophie Toscan du Plantier. These have become evident as a result of him being caught in lies by AGS and others. However, many of his deceptions have been exposed by Bailey himself.

On many important topics, Bailey has given several contradictory versions of what happened. When he gives three separate mutually exclusive descriptions of the same event then at least 2 are untrue. It is possible, even likely that all of them are untrue. A false alibi and many contradictory, almost ever-changing, versions mean that he is no stranger to truth-avoiding lies. He has lied to cover up what he did on the day the murder was discovered. In December 2022 Barry Roche of the Irish Times spoke to Sophie's uncle J P Gazeau. The uncle pointed out that Bailey had given conflicting evidence under oath. And at least one version, probably both were lies.

Irish Times 23.12.2022

Mr Gazeau said Mr Bailey also changed his story in relation to what he did once he got the call from Mr Cassidy, telling the libel action in 2003 that he proceeded to Dreenane in Toormore as he knew there was a French woman living near Alfie Lyons for whom he had done some gardening work.

"But at the case in Dublin in 2014, Mr Bailey suddenly introduces this element that he decided to go Jermyn's Post Office as the post-office would know what foreigners were living in the area, so he and Jules Thomas drove over by Sophie's house at Dreenane, just over the hill from Dunmanus Bay.

In May 2023 an account on Facebook pressed Bailey about his false alibi. He tried the usual nonsense to misdirect her. When he ran out of excuses he suddenly claimed that AGS cold case team had contacted him to arrange a meeting and he could say no more until he had spoken to them. This was a patent lie. Since this exchange, he has said he is still waiting for AGS to approach him for a meeting. He lies and then tells another lie to cover his lies.

19 May 2023 at 11:01

They are also false alibis because 1. Jules admitted it was false. 2. You changed your story completely from in bed all night to all the ins outs and locations. If the early statements were NOT FALSE then 1 and 2 would not have happened would they? We are both intelligent people we can draw logical conclusions. I did not expect you to respond immediately nor request it.

19 May 2023, 12:02

Emms whilst appreciating your contact and support
...Ive been contacted by Guards re Cold Review...I will
be answering their questions and no body elses

19 May 2023, 12:38

Today? Wow. In the last hour. That is such a coincidence
isn't it. That leaves 2 4 5 7.

I could say you could not make it up, but Bailey was always
doing so. The unadulterated truth eventually destroyed him.

Situational lies

These are the lies that Bailey spat out when he could not
remember what he had previously said about a topic or
wanted to give a quick answer that put a positive spin on
the subject being discussed. The adage that if you tell the
truth you don't need a good memory applies here. He did
not tell the truth and had told so many lies and falsehoods
that he could not remember what he had said. This is true
for important events regarding the murder of Sophie Toscan
du Plantier.

The issue of scratches is an important one. Sophie's
murderer likely received scratches from the briars at the
scene of the crime. For this reason, one would expect him
to be consistent in his statements about scratches. This
expectation of consistency is heightened by his boasts. He
spends 14 months producing 3 recordings – amount to a

derisory 2 hours of waffle – for his much-hyped podcast. He repeatedly made claims it was a meticulous examination of all the evidence. He insisted that no stone would be unturned. He asserted that it had been an exhausting endeavour. Given the self-promotion, one would expect him to be crystal clear on the subject of scratches. However, this turned out not to be the case. In the space of nine days, Bailey gives mutually exclusive versions of events. These may be added to several other of his scratch stories. It should also be noted that the timings he gave for cutting down a Christmas tree – that he claims led to his scratches – would mean he climbed up a tree and cut the top off in semi-darkness!

Never A Truer Word ✅ @truer word · 16 Oct   ...
Does Ian Bailey change his story from one week to another like this? Find out here youtube.com/live/C1Gcv2bnn...
#JusticeForSophieToscanduPlantier

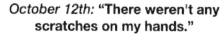

October 3rd: "Everyone saw I had scratches on my hand, the local Garda Superintendent when I went up to the crime scene to cover the story, another reporter and photographer with me. It was no big deal. They were there for all to see."

October 12th: "There weren't any scratches on my hands."

He gave interviews to different people and just told them a story that came to mind. If you were to ask him about the scratches he would more than likely come up with yet another version. New situation. No corroboration. There is no reason to trust his word on anything.

Earlier in this chapter it was shown how Bailey would claim a perfect memory or a poor memory depending on the situation and the reply that suits him at the time. Cometh the situation cometh the lie. Anything said by this man needs to be tested and verified. His story changes to back up whatever he is talking about in the moment. Do not assume he will stick to that narrative.

Victim narratives

Poor little Ian. His bullying and intimidation ploys became laughed at. His impotence and weakness were widely agreed upon. His personal power is rent asunder. People knew he lied about other people and his threats were empty. The failed bullying and 'threatening' are examples of him firing blanks. His last desperate throw of the dice has been to create fictitious victim narratives. He thought that journalists helping him to push these stories would result in people believing his woes. He did not see we didn't believe a word. They caused people to laugh.

He has claimed that forces were out to get him. He never specified who they were, Whether it was an individual, several separate individuals, or a coordinated group. Yet he claimed to know that 'someone' was after him. He stated that it had become necessary to hide the location of his home and his daily whereabouts. If you are being pursued by violent people that makes a lot of sense.

Once again there are reasons to question these tales told by the 'Bantry Billy liar'. First, there is a total lack of specifics that verify his fairy tales. This is reason enough to doubt the veracity of this victim narrative. There is one other reason we should not take these claims seriously. That is, he did not take his claims seriously.

At times when he has run with his life in danger narrative he had simultaneously posted his phone number and email address and invited strangers – most often unknown women – to 'WhatsApp' him. He had publicised when and where he could be found near Bantry and Schull markets. He has done TIKTOK videos looking down from his flat onto a recognisable Indian restaurant in Bantry. Indeed, concerning the open mic poetry event where he lied about people being ejected, he had earlier publicised on social media that he would be there. These are hardly the behaviours of a man in fear of his life. They point to a liar wanting sympathy. This is what happens when a narcissist tries to combine a 'people are out to get me' narrative with a self-publicity narrative. We could see it but Bailey and his chums believed his hype. He has claimed to have been stalked but without any evidence. He cries hate crime when people criticise him. The man could not stand up for himself so instead played the victim card with his lies. The recent saga of his potential eviction has been a further crass outburst from this cry-baby man-child. Typical headlines included: "The situation is causing me severe anxiety': Ian Bailey to be evicted from West Cork home."

The lazy man, wholly dependent on the Irish state to pay for his housing, utilities, food, booze, and toilet paper has known about the impending end of his tenancy for many months. He appeared to do nothing and then ran to the press with his poor 'anxious me' stories. During this period, he found the time to do his podcast, be vulgar to women online, and be charged for drunk- driving but not find accommodation, did not think he was paranoid, he was not afraid. The victim ploy gave him two things he desperately needed. First playing the victim gave him plenty of publicity. Several newspapers were happy to tell his tales of woe. It was just one extra way he could feed his narcissism. The second thing was it gave him a lever. He would extend the victim narrative to anyone who challenged him. He had no cogent arguments, his lies, insults, and bullying were no longer cutting through. He had lost his power. The big beast had become a meek mediocrity craving sympathy.

More recently there had been the heart attack saga. These were heart attacks that have still freed up Bailey to drive to the hospital, and give press and radio interviews about his victim state while referring to the murder case. It is thin gruel. While his heart problems may have stopped Bailey's blood circulation and stopped him breathing they did not stop him lying and giving press interviews. What he failed to understand was that people saw through his victimhood ploys. Indeed, people took pleasure in seeing how decrepit and desperate he had become.

In this chapter, I have not even considered the many people who have given evidence that contradicts the statements of Bailey. They include a dozen who have separately heard him confess, several who report that he said he knew Sophie, all the people making statements asserting that he and Thomas knew about the murder long before the time he claims he was officially told, the group of people who saw no scratches on him the night leading up to the murder. The people who attest to his lying are legion.

His former partner Jules Thomas is prominent among the people who contradicted Bailey. If just some of what these people say is true then he is guilty of many more lies. Those lies point to his involvement in Sophie's murder. Because many of us were tuned into his lying and exposed it he had become terrified of debating the facts. Instead, he hid in his hovel generating more puerile lies that can be shot down in moments. I wrote to Baliey in October about his lies:

October 24th A final prompt

Hi Mate,

a final prompt re my email of the 19th.

first I am delighted, though not surprised, that you have found no inaccuracies in the blog to date. This is not surprising because the sources I have used are your outputs.

In statements, articles, recorded interviews and social media communications.

In passing I note you have never been able to give the precise source for your podcast claim that on December 21st, 1996, a man " **had subsequently followed the French visitor up the road to her parked car in Ardnamanagh.**" With your journalist and academic lawyer hats on you can see that this could look like another lie. I have not seen any statement by Farrell or anyone else to that effect and in that detail. Is there a source or is it another lie?

You say you want the murderer of Sophie caught and want your name to be cleared as soon as possible. that would mean that you informed AGS immediately of the Ardnamanagh information. Did you do so?

I am, however, surprised you are scared to debate your case. Would John Wayne shout childish names, or lie about women or cower away like a wuss? Wayne was not a recreant who talked big then hid.

Put me to the test. Show me the evidence that any of the lies I describe is not so and I will withdraw it and apologise. Put me to the test. If you want to hunt me down why not meet me face to face and debate.

Cheers Mate

JPH

Bailey did not point out a single error

Whenever he communicated any type of information it could not be taken at face value. He was a prolific liar who lied for many reasons. When a man lies about inconsequential matters such as when he wrote a poem he will lie about anything. In the absence of strong corroborating evidence what he said had no credibility.

While his dishonesty has served him 'well' from moment to moment it has simultaneously chipped away at his integrity. To the point where it was in tatters. As the narcissist craves a public profile he must live in the public eye. This means his words and deeds are in the public domain and they are a matter of record. The more he said and wrote the more we could see his contradictions and falsehoods and lies. The more he was exposed.

We saw him. There was no escape.

How the attack on Bailey's lies worked

For most of his life Bailey got away with constant lying. threatening and bullying people. Then a few years ago a small group of decent people decided to challenge him. Bailey and his goons behaved appallingly but they could not deter the few people determined to tell the truth.

The more Bailey behaved in a vile way the more he was challenged. When he lied to cover his filth those lies were also called out.

This started to stress and exhaust Bailey. The more he pushed his falsehoods the more he got shot down. This was not a world he knew and it was hurting him.

He was trapped in a vicious spiral. To extricate himself his only tactics were to lie and bully people. When he did so the new lies and threats would be challenged. Yet he could not stop himself. He wanted to be a public figure.

The anecdotal definition of madness is 'doing the same thing and expecting new results. But Bailey was stuck and inflexible. He could not escape.

The man was now routinely mocked derided and disbelieved. He had no credibility and he knew it. He was psychologically running on empty. His attempts to lash out were pitiful. He was done.

Unable to cope with having his filth called out Bailey retreated to his dirty hovel and hid. His occasional public outbursts were error strewn and revealing.

In his hovel he ignored medical advice and drank and smoked and awaited his death. His life had been over for years.

2023 was to be Bailey's annus horribilis

CHAPTER **6**

Bailey's last full year 2023

Ian Bailey's last full year was one of utter failure and decline. All of it was of his own making. The 2022 exposure of his intellectual limitations, his cowardice, the weakness of his legal defence, and his moral turpitude were eclipsed by the events of 2023. In February 2023 I let him know that I would be in Co Cork later that month and that if he sought to carry out his desire to attack me, I would defend myself and call the Garda. I suggested that given our differences and his alleged complaints to AGS, we could both go to Skibbereen Police Station and voluntarily hand over our phones and computers so that they could be checked out. He appeared reluctant to do so. I told him I wanted to challenge his paedophilic interests. It had only a couple of weeks earlier that he had enjoyed watching the child masturbating on Twitter.

He told me where and when he would meet me on the Saturday. Close to the stall of a gifted carpenter and woodworker he personally knew and to a hot food stall. Through the morning I tweeted a few times where I was en route to Skibbereen such as the time I was going through Clonakilty. There was a stream of tweets by Bailey essential claiming he was there and waiting for me, or insulting me, and some so incoherent that they defied comprehension. He did not turn up. He was in his dirty little room, most likely drunk sending tweets while hiding away. He claimed I was being captured on CCTV. That one again 😵. He has chickened, again. Little wonder later in the year he would suffer heart problems, it was only the size of a pea.

I chatted with the carpenter, he knew Bailey well. He told me that quite unexpectedly Bailey had telephoned him the night before. He could tell me little else as Bailey was virtually incoherent. A man speaking to the carpenter said they very rarely saw Bailey. There was talk he had been banned from the market. When he did visit he stumbled around the place carrying a large sack of his books, He rarely sold any. On the whole, people gave him a wide berth and preferred him not to be there. He was rattled.

Has anybody seen Bailey's podcast?

The questions about the launch of Bailey's podcast continued through the early part of 2023. When would people get to hear episode one, promised in September 2022 then October, November and December 2022? This was followed by no-shows January and February. Every day he knew people would be on social media asking when it would be out. This running sore was the result of an inflated ego making big promises combined with mediocre talent and a poor work ethic. He had painted himself into a corner. The stress was of his own making and he was squirming.

The stress from his endless public flops had a two-pronged impact. He had a strong compulsion to try some huge gesture to put himself back in the game, while at the same time, the stress was weakening him and severely limiting his ability to deliver even a mediocre performance.

He was no longer the Marlon Brando contender; he was the bum. The punch-drunk out-of-shaped old boxer who thought he could still win the title. Claiming he could deliver the big knockout punch while falling over when getting into the ring. While 'punchy' he agreed to be interviewed for the Shattered Lives podcast. With no one there to throw in the towel, this would be a 'bloodbath.'

Shattered lives Shattered Defences

Bailey loved publicity. He would publicise every newspaper interview, radio tv, or podcast appearance. He would advertise their impending publication or broadcast; he would comment upon them and provide links to them. Following his Shattered Lives interview, for the first time, Bailey fell silent. It was like it never happened. Or more precisely he wished it had never happened.

He was right to feel that way. He was now physically and psychologically creaking. He appeared to be a dead man walking. The combination of the cold case review and the increasing pressure coming from a community who were no longer going to be cowed by the psychopath was getting too much for him. Individuals were running rings around him. He could not admit to his routine humiliations but they were eating away at him. His recent no-show with me and his farcical efforts with his podcast were taking a toll. His Shattered Lives performance was a car crash.

Part of the podcast focused on key elements of his involvement with the murder case. It set me on a line of research that pointed to him lying about the case repeatedly and knowing far more about Sophie's murder than he admitted to. The podcast was released on March 13th, 2023, It had likely been recorded 3 to 5 days before that.

Some key podcast observations

At the beginning of the recording, Bailey told the interviewer, Paul Healy, that 'hopefully' episode one of his podcast would be launched on St Patrick's Day. Only hopefully! He was incapable of giving a firm date, even just a few days before it was due to be available. This was yet another launch date spewed out by a serial incompetent. A deadline he could and would be pressed on. A deadline he could be called out on and mocked if he failed to achieve it. He had spent years bragging about how talented he was and how hopeless were his adversaries. Now the worm had turned and this biter was being bit.

He implied that the 'Sophie' case led to his breakup with Jules Thomas. He stated it was a natural process whereby couples grow apart. When asked if there were strains in the relationship he said, 'Not particularly'. He was lying. Their separation was very acrimonious and he had to be forced out of the house. Within days, in a press interview, Thomas spelled out how lazy and obnoxious he was, and the extraordinary lengths she had to go to get him out of her home. His reluctance to go was not based on love but on his dependence on Thomas, his desire to use women, and his inability to pay his way.

The lies Bailey told about Thomas led to her reply. For too long the falsehoods put out by him had gone unchallenged. But things had changed, he was struggling more and more with the weight of the truth. This was a new world for him and he did not like it.

Bailey told Healy that in terms of the murder it had been accepted by the DPP that he had nothing to do with it. That was a clear-cut lie on a particularly important matter. They never said that. It is not their job to do that. There is no doubt he lied. This was a significant error by him. He tried to explain and justify his assertion but he was floundering. He had been caught in a lie. Not only that but he had been recorded when doing so. When he said such things to small groups of ill-informed 'groupies' they believed him. When he asserted this falsehood in a bar it would often be greeted as fact. What he said was untrue and he knew it and he knew he had slipped up.

A couple of years earlier he would have been able to manoeuvre his way through an interview. This time he was mentally and physically weaker. He had made the error of going onto a high-quality podcast with a journalist with an excellent understanding of the case. His vanity and hunger for a high profile had led him into dangerous territory.

The interview returned to the events of 23.12.96 and Bailey said he heard of the death at 1.40 pm when Eddie Cassidy telephoned him at home. He said he was told the victim was a Foreign national possibly French, explaining he had recently found his notebooks where he recorded this point. The reference to finding notebooks and those notebooks recording what he claims Cassidy told him were new items of information. This slip raised important questions about Bailey's dishonesty. He told Jules Thomas that the deceased was French (not a foreign national, possibly French). He told the Garda in his earliest statements that he knew where to find the deceased because he knew a French woman lived in Dreenane. He provided a statement to the Garda that Eddie Cassidy told him the deceased was French, though Cassidy denied it. Hereto he did not refer to the victim being a foreign national. Furthermore, soon after speaking to Eddie Cassidy, he told photographic editor, Padraig Bierne, that the dead woman was, you've guessed it, French.

Bailey had told listeners that he had a written record of what Cassidy had told him. Yet, in the 10 seconds between speaking to Cassidy and telling Thomas about the dead woman, he wanted everyone to believe he had completely forgotten that he had been told she was a foreign national. No sane person would buy that bill of goods. Under pressure, he was leaking bits of information that damaged his defence.

He was not leaking like a dripping tap or even a sieve. This was a bursting dam. It was about to get worse.

At this point, he stated that he and Thomas set off for the Toormore Post Office. En route, they happened to meet Shirley Foster. Bailey said it was Foster, a neighbour of Sophie, who told him the Police were swarming around the cottages in Dreenane. This led to Bailey allegedly postponing his visit to the Post Office and driving to Dreenane. To the casual listener, this all sounded plausible. To people with a detailed knowledge of the case, this was a huge change in the story originally told by Bailey. It meant he was telling conflicting stories and contradicting himself on important aspects of the case.

This was something I locked on to. In all his early statements Bailey told the Garda he knew where to go to find the dead woman, later identified as Sophie. He drove straight to the scene of the crime. He met Foster halfway down Dreenane Lane. This lane led only to the cottages where Sophie was found. There would be no other reason to be driving down this narrow, off-road, lane. Only after briefly speaking to officers at the scene of the crime did he and Thomas travel to the Post Office. He had known exactly where to go long before bumping into Foster.

Thomas corroborated the original Bailey version. Going straight to the scene of the crime, meeting Foster on Dreenane Lane, and later visiting the post office. In a later statement, Thomas explained that they went to the post office to get the name of the dead woman. Shirley Foster corroborated the original Bailey version. She met him and Thomas on Dreenane Lane as she was driving away from the cottages and he was coming towards her. Bailey was already going to the scene of the crime when they met. In later statements, Foster re-affirmed where she met him and angrily challenged his changed versions of what happened.

The Shattered Lives version was damning. Bailey wanted people to forget all he had said in early statements, everything said by Jules Thomas and Shirley Foster. He wanted everyone to forget that he immediately knew where to find the dead body of Sophie and to instead accept his latest lies. A group of us would not forget. We would not let it go.

I would go on to write a detailed analysis of Bailey's statements to the Garda, his written accounts of what happened that day, and his statements in interviews, including the Shattered Lives interview. The analysis was warmly welcomed by ASSOPH the French organisation committed to getting justice for Sophie. ASSOPH submitted a copy of the research to the AGS cold case review team. I posted my findings on my blog. A short version and a thirty-two-page long version showing how he systematically changed his story over more than twenty years. It showed how he nearly succeeded in hiding the truth. I sent copies to him, and he neither acknowledged them nor denied them but he knew all about them.

There were other slip-ups and insights into the mind of Bailey. He appeared reluctant to condemn the bestial murder of Sophie. It appeared a strange response if he was an innocent man. His decision to not comment on the podcast was also to that point unique. Many people on social media platforms repeatedly asked him about what he had said in the episode and why he had been silent afterward. Several months later people would continue to ask him about the podcast and recommend it to others. This was the last time he had the nerve to be interviewed by a well-prepared journalist. He had lost his nerve and he would never get it back.

His errors under pressure were now revealing his culpability. He was demolishing the shaky foundations of his legal defence. This was causing him to experience ever more stress and he had no answers. Each day the level of stress appeared to increase with no prospect of it being alleviated. What had been a platform where he could feed his ego had become somewhere where he would be continuously undermined.

Bailey returns to his grooming DMs

One thing that Ian Bailey could do was make those who opposed him laugh. Not through his sense of humour you understand. While calling someone a turd in a junior school may get the occasional laugh, an adult repeatedly calling people turds over and over is not too amusing. While his world was in tatters he managed to bring much merriment with a tweet he posted on March 12th, 2023.

Ian Kenneth Bailey BCL, LLB, LLM (UCC)
@IanKennethBail1

Ye invented Vagzilla...Hope the Larbottomy works 😂 😂 😂

4:09 PM · Mar 12, 2023 · **458** Views

Long after he had been taken apart by the woman who challenged his grooming activity. Long after he had made so many contradictory excuses for his grooming DMs. Bailey posted the above tweet concerning me . It had been nine months since his vile attempts to groom Vagzilla. Maybe he was still chuntering about his cowardly no-show in Skibbereen in late February. Whatever the reason he was now back to his claim that I had catfished him.

He was so confused that he had not thought things through. He was still reflecting on his dreadful performance in the Shattered Lives podcast. If what he said about me had been true, it was still him who sent grooming DM's. He had DM'd advice on how a girl could deceive her family and run away to West Cork for sex with him. The DMs about his penis, his sexual preferences, and his use of courgettes were all his own. It had been his choice to send a photo of his underwhelming penis to a stranger!

If that were not funny enough it occurred to us that in March 2023 he believed all his DMs may have gone to me and not to a 15-year-old child. He was telling Holzer about his uncontrollable erections. 😂 He had told Holzer he wanted him to sit on his face. 😂 In his mind Ian Bailey had sent a photo of his 'thirsty mouth' to Holzer, later asking Holzer what he thought of Bailey's pinky. 😂 The sheer torment of the man. 😂

Turning into a tramp and a bin dipper

Bailey once looked healthy and well-dressed. All this was due to Jules Thomas. She fed him and clothed him. Soon after she had got him out of her home the cocky and aggressive man went into decline. He appeared unable to live healthily and hygienically. In a very short time, he drifted effortlessly into becoming a vagrant. This did not go unnoticed, the man who mocked people about their appearance was now going to be on the receiving end. The persistent teasing and taunting of Bailey took on a life of their own. People pointed out how Bailey was often seen scavenging or half-eaten sandwiches and other foodstuffs in waste bins. He picked up names like the tramp and the Bantry bin-dipper. Others would tweet stock photos of tramps rummaging in bins while referring to Bailey. He was photographed shuffling around Bantry looking like a tramp and pushing an empty supermarket trolley [This can be found on the website Pervert in the Hills].

There had been TIKTOK videos showing Bailey in Bantry drunk as a lord. He would be trying to scrounge free drinks or cigarettes. He was openly mocked. People did not like the man. He was often caught short in the evenings in Bantry. This was due to that hideous combination of too much alcohol, a weak bladder and only being able to walk slowly. The shop doorways between bars Bailey would frequent and his flat paid the price.

Prison life

Ian Bailey followed what was being said about him on social media, He had gone from being a man who would bully and threaten anyone and everyone on social media, to being someone who blocked everyone. He was not only a coward in the real world he was a coward in the virtual world. Knowing that he read what was being said about him prompted people to raise topics he would likely read. On more than one occasion there was speculation about what life would be like in prison for him. The consensus was that warders and prisoners would not take too well to a woman murderer, a man with a sexual interest in children, or a man who insulted Irish people saying they were unintelligent and uncultured. The same man who was on record insulting Irish accents and the man who took millions out of the Irish economy and put nothing in. It would not be good.

The common reactions to people like him would include adulterated food and drink, frequent loss of or damage to spectacles and false teeth, and excessive verbal abuse. Then there would be the violence and extreme sexual abuse. This would range from a straightforward punch through to anal rape with sharp implements. These truths were disturbing to him and his acolytes. The social media platforms became an ever greater source of despair for him.

And onwards

The year got progressively worse. The fallout from Shattered Lives was to rumble on until Bailey passed. As we will see later, the 'In my own words' podcast became a running sore throughout 2023. In it, Bailey would continue to alienate people around him. He would confirm his inadequacies and weaknesses. Moreover, he would let slip vital information more than once that would point to his culpability.

Other developments were reported throughout the year and occasionally from surprising sources. On October 4th Senan Molony reported that the most advanced DNA recovery technologies were going to be used by investigators of the Sophie Toscan du Plantier murder. These included the use of the MVAC system that was able to retrieve DNA from sources that had previously been inaccessible. Officers who had successfully solved cases after decades were now focussing on Sophie's case with all the resources they needed. Just over three weeks later further progress was reported.

A much more surprising source was an article by John Kierans at the end of October. In most cases this journalist had tended to author articles telling us that he was launching his latest get-rich-quick gimmick, or yet another 'I am a victim story' or a story from his ' they are evicting me,' saga. All dull stuff that offered a little nourishment for the Bailey ego.

Later in the year, Kierans would author many articles about Bailey's heart attacks and health scares. There would be interviews from his bed, stories about his treatments along with Bailey hoping to live long enough to see himself cleared. I am sure that was a sentiment that moved the odd person. More accurately it would have moved only very odd persons. Once Bailey died Kierans was one of a group of journalists who within days, were able to tell us just how sad, miserable, twisted, tormented, impoverished, and weird he had become.

However, on October 30th the article opened with 'Cops are increasingly confident that they will finally get justice for Sophie Toscan du Plantier'. A senior Police Officer told the journalist they believed they knew who had murdered Sophie and that the person lived locally and knew her. The officer added that a cast iron case was being put together that could be taken to court. There was a belief that the cold case team already had enough evidence to justify a trial. They insisted they had a huge amount of circumstantial evidence which they were convinced would stand up in court.

Kierans explained that the Gardai regarded Bailey as ' a person of interest' and that he had been convicted for Sophie's murder in France in 2019. The cold case officers had not spoken to Bailey about the murder. Perhaps more surprisingly John Kierans, did not speak to him about those developments. Usually, he and Bailey appeared to speak freely on most topics but this time, nothing.

The article told him that the officers did not believe the murderer was dead or overseas. This showed they did not accept the stories of a dead rogue cop or a German national who had committed suicide, nor all the suggestions that the killer was a hitman. This was exerting significant stress on him.

A week before Christmas, Ralph Riegal wrote for the Irish Independent that the Gardai were making "significant progress" in the case. Riegal had written a book on the case and is a journalist with a formidable reputation as a real crime writer. He reported that the detectives had not made a single case-breaking discovery. Instead, the officers had examined new material and built ' a very strong and very detailed case around circumstantial evidence.' The detectives were taking a twin-track approach. There was both a continuance of the original investigation and a cold case review in which everything was being re-examined and subjected to the most up-to-date forensic techniques. Merry Christmas Mr Bailey!

"I was happy in a haze of a drunken hour" Morrissey

What had become increasingly clear was Bailey's withdrawal from public life. It was akin to a transgressing politician retiring to the country to, 'have more time with their family.' These people tended to live in opulence and obscurity henceforward. For Bailey there was no family, nobody much cared for him. He lived in squalor in a tiny flat he could not afford. All of this he would reluctantly tolerate, but the obscurity and his obvious failure as a man would have been unbearable. Yet bearing it was his only option.

The continued drinking and smoking after his heart attacks would prevent him from getting the treatment he needed while simultaneously worsening his condition. But to remain sober meant he had to face the truth. The truth of his failures, his loss of control, and his impending arrest. He was trapped. When drunk he was destroying his body and in bitter torment. When sober the harsh realities ate him. Oh dear, such a shame. No longer was he 'happy in a haze of a drunken hour'. Being drunk may have slightly taken the edge off his despair but that was all.

Bailey is in terminal decline

As I looked at Ian Bailey's career record I quickly concluded that it was not a career and he was an underachiever. A life of mediocrity is little comfort for most people. For a malignant narcissist, this is a disaster. How could you wish to be the God of all things when you could not hold a job?

In Gloucester, he was lucky to be in the right place at the right time when a major political and British intelligence scandal broke. That improved his profile at the same time as he briefly married into money. Quickly everything fell apart and with a divorce settlement he went to London 'to make his fortune.' However, there, he could not cut it. He was there for years but it is impossible to find a body of work where he is the sole author or lead journalist. He lasted in the city until his divorce settlement ran out.

He claimed to have left 'Fleet Street' because he could not stomach the Maxwell and Murdoch approach to journalism. It is a touching story, one that is unbelievable. First, because the tabloid journalism he complained about had been in situ for decades. Second, he set a great store by his work at the Sunday Times which was far from a tabloid. Third, none of the national papers would give him a full-time job. He was not good enough,

The fourth reason to disbelieve Bailey is the funniest. He says he objected to gutter journalism. This is the man who allegedly forged insurance policies in his wife's name and was said to have tried to import illegal pornography into the UK. He was a pathological liar, a bully, a beater of women. He had for decades enjoyed hardcore pornography and had a sexual interest in children. Yet he wants people to believe he was taking a moral stand, Does anyone believe that? Me neither.

He did not leave London for UK provincial newspapers or seek journalistic work when he goes to Ireland, instead, he takes up a series of cash in hand, temporary jobs in locations across the country. In many cases, he has changed his name. The final job where he worked for forty-plus hours a week was in a fish factory on the Atlantic coast in the early 1990s. From then until 2024 he did not have a regular job. He did not pay taxes into the Irish system.

After leaving the fish factory Bailey moved in with and was dependent on Jules Thomas. When he was asked to leave the Thomas home he was dependent on money from the Irish state. He was incapable of supporting himself. During his time with Thomas, he was awarded three law degrees. He claimed to be an 'academic lawyer'. In reality, he was incapable of doing anything with those degrees.

The deeply narcissistic man had been a flop. There were no sustained achievements. He was, despite his degrees, a slow and mediocre thinker. He was not quick-witted and despite the myths he created about himself he had precious little charm. In his time in West Cork, his entire reputation was built on him playing the victim in the Sophie case plus his endless lying and bullying.

In the last few years of his life, every last vestige of his positive sense of self was being disassembled.

His last throw of the dice would be his gift to posterity. His 'In my Own Words' podcast.

CHAPTER 7

Bailey In my own words 1 – How not to make a podcast

Bailey had been well and truly stomped from April to June 2022. He decided to put all his eggs in one basket at around that time. The big man was going to produce his podcast. He was going to create a podcast that would slay all his opponents, fill his pockets with money, and make him king of the castle. If ever there needed to be an indication that Ian Bailey was delusional this was it.

As a malignant narcissist, he was not one to work stealthily. He would not work hard and with rigour alongside an international team of elite experts for nine months, then announce it with great fanfare. Not Ian. He ran to the press ill-informed and ill-prepared with no appreciation of his significant inadequacies. It was just one big ' Look at me aren't I the business' trip. Many people would see it as a sad failure talking himself up. It was much more. There were many times when he would announce his latest get-rich-quick gimmick. The shout-outs on TIKTOK, his video, the novel about trolls, his moob-exposing t-shirts, the big documentary he would create, concert tours, and of course his carved wooden penises. All of them flopped.

The 'In my own words' podcast was on a different scale altogether. He was apt to say it would be his legacy, his gift to posterity. How future generations might better understand him. Furthermore, he expected future generations to perceive him as innocent and a great poet. And more importantly a man of means.

By this podcast, you shall know him. This turned out to be true, The podcast was a car wreck. A disaster and (sorry folks) a plodcast. In the previous chapter, you learned how this all ends. Bailey claims it has tens of thousands of downloads and positive feedback almost off the scale. It ends with Bailey producing weapons-grade lies on an industrial scale. His 'self-predicted' biggest success became his largest flop. He would prove himself talentless and a bore. He would make slip-ups that showed his guilt and he would lose money on the deal. That was the real Bailey. Had he taken out a series of front-page newspaper adverts saying "Ian Bailey is a talentless drunk who could not find his arse with two hands, a map, and a couple of full-length mirrors" it would have been less damaging than his podcast – and far more amusing.

It begins

The launch of the first episode had been flagged up many times by Bailey. It became a running joke as people laughed as deadlines came and went. It was to be Summer 2022, then Autumn then December, January, a few times in February up to 3 or 4 times in March, and finally(drum roll) in April episode 1 appeared with a whimper. What an utter shambles.

How could Bailey get so much so wrong? On more than one occasion people have been told by him that he has crack teams of cyber specialists & tech experts. None of these people could advise Bailey on how to get his episode on Spotify. Nor could they sort out his website. This might be filed under: Bailey couldn't stop himself lying and thought we had not noticed. 😂

The announcement

> **Ian Bailey compares himself to John Wayne with new podcast to tell 'nothing but the truth'**
>
> **IAN BEGLEY** on **2ND JUNE 2022** Evoke.ie Excerpts
>
> Ian Bailey is planning to produce his own podcast and documentary in a bid to reveal the 'trial, tribulations and torture… for a crime, I didn't commit'.
>
> Speaking to the Irish Daily Mail, Mr Bailey said that his new project, entitled Ian Bailey: In His Own Words, will leave no stone unturned. 'It'll be a six-part podcast,' he said. 'The first episode will see me reply to all of the false allegations and nonsense that has been uttered about me over the past 25 years

'Other people started to write books, making all sorts of defamatory allegations…. I'm now in a John Wayne state of mind and am going to get them back at their own game.'

Further episodes will see Mr Bailey talk about how he ended up in Ireland and the events leading up to Christmas 1996. He added: 'I will be naming and shaming people and if they want to challenge me they're very welcome to do it. Everything I say will be the truth, the whole truth and nothing but the truth.'

The final episode will depict the Cork resident's life over the past 12 months, including how his relationship came to an end, becoming homeless and 'resurrecting myself again'. He will also give listeners the chance to ask 'reasonable and rational questions' and answer these in the last episode. Mr Bailey said he is exploring the possibility of crowd-funding the project online.

After the podcast is released by the end of this summer, Mr Bailey said he plans on making a documentary about his life. He remarked: 'I've got a very good idea how I want it to turn out and have hours of unused footage that was shot for the Jim Sheridan documentary last year.'

In the beginning was Bailey's word. This was not a good start! He promises six episodes. In one early article, he said each would be two hours long. He is clear that in episode one he would specifically address what he called the 'false allegations. This would be followed by four episodes (2-5) that he said would address how he ended up in Ireland through to the events of December 1996. On day one Bailey was astonishingly underprepared and vague. It was almost as if he was doing his life's most important work off the cuff. In the final episode, he would cover his last 12 months! Wait a minute. When read the article I burst out laughing. According to him episode 5 finished in December 1996 and episode 6 would cover June 2021 to June 2022. That left a hole of 24 years. Surely Ian Begley must have burst out laughing or at least asked him about a huge hole in the timeline.

Those people addicted to the full range of Bailey products would have been delighted to see that as soon as episode one was launched he would be making a documentary, presumably about himself. Naturally but unsurprisingly, they would be disappointed to learn that this was another boastful lie from the man.

What has he been doing for eleven weeks? – The Mallon article

In August 2022 Bailey gave Sandra Mallon an interview for the Irish Mirror. It was unknown how many months of meticulous planning he had put into the project before his June 2nd launch. The interview came eleven weeks after the high-profile launch. It was impossible to avoid the question 'What had he been doing for eleven weeks?' My money would always be on him dithering and drinking too much.

He had said the first episode would be launched at the end of summer. Surely by August the first recording would be in the can and being prepared for going public?

Eleven weeks later things had changed. Now the six-part podcast had become a five-part version and Bailey is forced to acknowledge that he has not got the expertise and experience to make his podcast content. Why did he not know his limitations and admit to them in the beginning? Probably because he thinks he is perfect until he has to do something. For him, reality was so inconvenient, a slap in the face.

He never explained why he cut his audio biography down from 6 to 5 episodes. He admitted to not having the money required to make the podcast work. Once again it appears that he had come up with a 'bright idea', not planned & costed it, and gone off half-cocked. This seems to have left him floundering and making little progress. His claim that he would have the first episode out by the end of summer was not the product of a proper business plan. Instead, it is a date picked out of the air by a man already out of his depth and likely drunk at the time.

The claim that his podcast with be forensically rigorous is emphasised. He says he will go through everything in minute detail. There is a lot to get through but he decided he could now do it in five episodes rather than six.

[This next paragraph is untrue but does allow for a bit of dramatic effect] I had spent many sleepless nights since June the second. On other occasions, I would wake from some hellish nightmare screaming " What about the two civil trials in 2003 and 2014!" (even when terrified by a night terror I am spot on with dates) or "How will Bailey address the conclusions of the 2018 GSOC report in his podcast." Not bad ey?

At this early point, there could already be questions about the project. He says he will be rigorous. But could he be relied upon in terms of anything he asserted or promised? His record in general says not. His actions were more consistent with a spur-of-the-moment idea coming to mind. Bailey then ran to the press with his grandiose promises based in part on his ludicrously high opinion of his skills and work ethic. If the project was not broken it was creaking.

Ian Bailey looks for help to make his own podcast called 'Ian Bailey: In His Own Words'

By <u>Sandra Mallon</u> 17 AUG 2022 Irish Mirror

Excerpts

The 64-year-old – who was the chief suspect in the murder of Sophie Toscan Du Plantier – revealed on his social media he was looking to find an experience podcaster to help him with his new venture.

He said he wants to call the five-part series, Ian Bailey In His Own Words.

He said: "Hi I am seeking the assistance of an experienced podcaster to assist me with my own five-part podcast Ian Bailey In His Own Words. Email 107867433@umail.ucc.ie"

> He said at the time: "I am trying to be creative and get on with my own podcast. I'm trying to make the money I need to make the podcast.
>
> "I am making slow progress with that, but that's just the way of productions.
>
> "The podcast is going to be under the working title of 'Ian Bailey in his own words'. Basically, I'm going to go through everything from day one and address everything false that's been said and have my say."

Approaching Christmas September to November 2022 and the rot is setting in

At first reading of his early message, it appeared that Ian was 'on it.' He told a friend the episodes would go out fortnightly. A few days later he was telling his TIKTOK followers that he had just started recording. Bailey confidently stated that episode one would be available before the end of 2022. This meant something he promised to deliver in 3 months would be released six months later.

His timings and deadlines were chaotic. This meant his whole enterprise was erratic and poorly managed.

On October 21st, his friends' fans and followers were told that from then onwards there would be a weekly podcast update. There was only one further video that appeared to be a formal update. He managed one weekly update over the next 35 weeks. This was yet another 'bright idea' blurted out but never delivered.

In November, the unraveling of Bailey comes front and centre. On the 17th he said he was well into episodes 1 and 2, with number one pretty well perfected, Yet in September he told the public episode one was being recorded! He admits that the creation of the podcast was an awful lot more work than he had anticipated. For me, this pointed to him over-rating his own talents and work ethic. At the same time, it reinforces the conclusion that his original and later plans were inadequate.

Four days later on the 21st, he repeats his view that episode one has been perfected. He adds that the following week episode 1 will be recorded. The same episode he said was recorded in September. Though Bailey is characteristically vague as he states he is hopeful it will be the following week. He lacks any precision in his thinking. He tells his TIKTOK listeners that episodes 2 and 3 are 'coming together' – whatever that means – then on the same day he puts out another video saying that he is perfecting episodes 3 and 4. Until this point there had been no mention of episode 4, then suddenly it is being perfected. This is chaotic. He also hints that there may be more than 4 episodes.

On November 30th he explained that the sound engineer was perfecting, presumably, episode 1 which would be available in the New Year. When in the new year remained a mystery. He explained that there would be four episodes and no others.[Spoiler alert] The first episode eventually goes live in late April 2023. That is a hell of a lot of perfecting! [Further spoiler alert, the finished product was not perfect]

He claimed to have thousands of friends fans and followers. He repeatedly claimed to have tech teams and teams of experts working with him. Yet not a single person pointed out to him his constant contradictions. Sometimes he would give mixed and confusing messages on the same day. One wondered just how many friends and expert teams he had.

SEPT 16TH TWITTER	Asked how often episodes would be released IKB – Every two weeks
SEPT 21ST TT	Just started recording Available before the end of the year
OCT 21ST TT	WEEKLY PODCAST UPDATE Nothing much to say
NOV 17TH TT	Well into episodes one and two One pretty well-perfected Awful lot more work than I anticipated

NOV 20TH	Got his writing mojo back
TT	One pretty well-perfected
	Recording next week hopefully
	Episodes 2 and 3 coming together
NOV 20TH	I am perfecting scripts 3, 4 possibly more episodes
	[Refers to a sound technician]
NOV 30TH	Podcast update
TT	Recording engineer perfecting recording
	Will be available in the new year
	It will be a four-parter

The end of 2022 looms and not an episode has been launched: December 2022

In December 2022 Bailey had already overrun his deadline for episode one. He had overrun the end of summer by a considerable margin. The big news was that the episode pencilled in for the beginning of autumn had just been recorded in the last days of November. Bailey was now overrunning into the next year. But there was more. His six-episode 'audio biography,' his Magnus opus, had first slipped down to 5 episodes and now it was only four.

He did reveal that episode one would be free and the others would come at a price. This was his biggest business idea ever. The product would be 24-carat Bailey. His thoughts and words would come at a price. A price he hoped would make him a pot full of money. Perhaps then he would pay off his legal debts? I'm kidding.

He tells Ali Bracken that he has finished episodes 2 and 3 adding that recording is due to continue 'this week or next'. This seemed unnecessarily vague. Surely he would know specific times and dates? Maybe not. A common observation of Bailey is his interminable vagueness. This week or next, early, or late next month, the end of summer. It indicates a feckless undisciplined mind. I cannot recall a single journalist insisting that Bailey be specific.

Ian Bailey is recording a podcast on Sophie Toscan du Plantier murder in West Cork

Ali Bracken independent 04 December 2022 Excerpts

Ian Bailey has recorded a podcast that will detail his life before and after the murder of Frenchwoman Sophie Toscan du Plantier in West Cork in 1996.

An audio engineer is currently editing the first of four episodes of *Ian Bailey: In his Own Words*, which was recorded last Wednesday.

The journalist-turned-poet said he expects the "professionally produced" podcast will be released in stages, early in the new year.

"The first episode is about my early life in England and has been recorded. The second and third concern my life after I moved to Ireland, including the events leading up to and the aftermath of Christmas 1996."

The Englishman says he has written the script for episodes two and three of his podcast, and recording is due to continue this week or next.

He added that he will release the first podcast for free to "pique interest", and there will likely be a monetary fee to listen to the remaining three episodes.

"It will focus on how I became the lead journalist reporting on the death of Ms Toscan du Plantier and everything that followed after that.

Whereby the end of summer becomes the end of February! The shifting sands of Ian Bailey's timelines

On January 10th Bailey informs his followers that episode 1 is recorded. Is this the same episode that he said was recorded at the end of November? He adds that episode 2 will be done later this week or early next week (another vague timescale). Is this the same episode 2 he told Ali Bracken was being recorded in early December? The man is a walking talking car crash. He was a truth-free zone.

It was not until sixteen days later that he declared that he had just finished recording episode 2. He always overruns.

He says episode 2 will be available in March. Four days later he pops up again to say that tomorrow he will be recording (drum roll) episode 2.

DEC 9TH TT	I'm making progress It will happen it won't be until January or February [Why so long? Recording in the can November 29th!! What is the contract will the engineer how long does he need?}
2023	
JAN 10TH TT	Episode 1 recorded Episode 2 will be recorded later this week or early next week (what happened early Dec?)
JAN 26TH TT	Just finished episode 2 (recording) about 45 minutes Available in March (not 1 hour?)
JAN 30TH TT	Recording the second episode tomorrow(?)

January came and went and still no podcast. What was Ian Bailey doing with his time? He was unwilling or unable to work so he could work on his podcast 24/7. At the beginning of February, there was another typical Bailey article. He offered another launch date. It was to be 'before the end of February.' He is being interviewed in early February, he has been working on it for close to eight months, but is incapable of giving a specific date, again.

He stated for the first time that he will no longer be interviewed in his podcasts. Instead, he will deliver a monologue. This can be filed under things he did not plan or announce at the beginning.

The excuse he gives for this change is he is being 'true to his lone wolf status.' This is something that has never been mentioned before. That he is lonely or cannot afford an interviewer would have been more believable. There was also the first mention of Ianbailey.net. Presumably, this would be the platform through which customers could pay for the downloads of episodes 2 3, and 4. He was going to set up a system for managing the transactions.

His final comment was "I'm having my say and I'm recording it for posterity." If it turns out to be a magnificent podcast posterity is a good thing for him. If it is a piece of mindless drivel, not so good for Mr B.[Spoiler alert – I am saying nothing, you will just have to guess at the outcome!]

February 2nd, 2023

Rebecca Fisher Extra live Excerpts

Ian Bailey has revealed he is releasing his 'much anticipated' audio biography, describing it as 'long awaited and keenly anticipated'.

'Ian Bailey: In His Own Words' is set to be released before the end of February, with the former journalist taking to social media to promote it.

Taking to Twitter to announce the upcoming podcast, Mr Bailey wrote: 'Coming Soon….My long awaited and keenly anticipated audio biography.'

When quizzed by a follower about the format of the project, he added; 'So the original plan was to do as an extended interview…but tru (sic) to my Lone Wolfe startus (sic) it will just be my voice…first ep will become available FREE from all podcast platforms further episodes will be available directly from.my ianbailey.net.'

Speaking to The Irish Sun about the impending release, Bailey added; 'Things are just the way they are. But the important thing for me in this is that I'm having my say and I'm recording it for posterity.'

FEB 6TH TT	First episode will be available free at the end of the month "all being well"
FEB 17TH TT	Re episode 3. It's very tough Introduction out by end of month Then March episode 2
FEB 22ND TT	"so, it is coming together at long last" Should be available at the end of the month

Ian Bailey says he 'will leave no stone unturned' in his podcast on Sophie Toscan du Plantier murder

Ali Bracken

Sun 26 Feb 2023 at 02:30 Excerpts

Ian Bailey will release the first part of his new podcast Ian Bailey: In His Own Words next week. It will detail his life before and after the murder of Frenchwoman Sophie Toscan du Plantier in west Cork in 1996.

Bailey, the chief suspect in the unsolved murder, has enlisted the services of an audio engineer and the introductory episode will be released **next week.**

Episodes one and two, each an hour long, will then be released in March and will be available on all major podcast platforms, he added. The journalist-turned-poet said he expects the "professionally produced" podcast will have four episodes in total and possibly a bonus fifth one.

The introduction and episode one will be released free of charge, and the rest of the series can be listened to for a "small fee" and purchased on Bailey's website.

"This is not about money, this is about me telling my own story in my own words, for the first time. I'm hoping that the introduction we are due to release next week will pique people's interest. I will leave no stone unturned and no turd unstirred. I will be addressing everything," he said.

> "I would expect interest could be quite high, considering how much interest there was in the two documentaries that were released last year on Sky and Netflix. This is my audio autobiography," he said. The first episode focuses on his early life growing up in the UK before he relocated to Ireland in 1991.

Nothing came out at the end of February. Then nothing came out at the end of March. He finally managed to get something out on April 24th, 2023. Nine months and 22 days to produce one podcast. It was only 33.55 minutes long including the long silences.

APRIL 3RD TT	Podcast delayed. Sound engineer Mark had a very nasty motorcycle accident. For a reason never explained Bailey says he will have to re-record the episodes.
APRIL 24TH	Episode 1 launched

The project ended in August 2023. The six-part podcast was to be his big earner and his legacy. He claimed that it would demolish the case against him and settle scores with a variety of people. The podcast would be rigorous dealing with things point by point. There was to be a website and a documentary following straight after the podcast. Well, it did not turn that way. There were only three episodes in the podcast with a total playing time of under two hours. There was no website and no payment system because there was not a single sale.

He said the project cost him money. There was no pot of gold at the end of this rainbow. The legacy is clear, he was completely out of his depth. It was one more of his big Walter Mitty ideas that ended up an embarrassing failure. It is what happens when a project is fuelled by hubris rather than talent and hard work.

Now we can move on to the content of the podcast episodes.

[Spoiler alert – oh come on, really, do I have to spell it out?]

CHAPTER 8

Bailey In my own words 2 - Is that all there is?

I have never won an international mental arithmetic competition so I will not attempt to quantify the number of times Bailey has changed his story, changed key details, or contradicted himself. The changes are legion. This means that much of what he says about the murder of Sophie Toscan du Plantier cannot be believed or trusted. Indeed, after so many 180-degree switches one might do better to ignore him completely. He has done an excellent job of discrediting himself.

He had made a complete fool of himself in the Shattered Lives podcast. He probably thought that without someone questioning him, he could present his best case, error-free. He announced the podcast in June 2022 and delivered a derisory 30 minutes over nine and a half months later. All that time to produce a 'half-finished' meandering episode. That works out at less than one minute of content per week. This was from a man who insisted he was an excellent journalist. He frequently spoke of 'perfecting' his episodes. The production had no music at the beginning and the end. There are no acknowledgments of people involved with the recording. Occasionally words are indistinct. His pontificating may stop mid-sentence. Such as "…no people on earth are more aware of the principle of independent."

What did he mean? I doubt anyone cares much what he was trying to say. But it is a pitiful piece of work all the same.

He thought he was presenting himself in a positive light when stating he was the author, presenter, director, and producer of his 30-minute 'Magnus Opus'. Wrong! In truth, it showed us that he could not write, present, direct, or produce. A full house of failure. It was a case study on how not to create a podcast.

The content produced by the self-regarding fantasist will come as no surprise to people who follow his social media outpourings. After all the 'honing and perfecting' of the Own Words script for over nine months the first episode included phrases and words like:

- he sent his lad Jesus
- I became a little Jesus boy
- From a special book called the bible
- Nooky
- We subsequently became entangled
- I made a little puddle
- a flock of crows
- Charlie boy
- womanly needs

His editor was completely out of his depth (I think we all suspect Ian did his editing). There is so much trivia and imprecision. He cannot remember when he recently met his sister. He says a friend of one of the girls, Ariana, was at the house on 22.12.96 when she did not arrive there until the afternoon of the 23rd. This is lazy and illustrates his disinterest in accuracy and contempt for his listeners. Not surprisingly he significantly underreported the beatings and violence aimed at Jules Thomas.

If he is to be believed he was a dim student who only managed to get 4 'O' (ordinary) levels by the age of 17. Boys at his school would be expected to get 7 to 10 'O' levels at 16 with some taken at 15. The expectation would be 4 'A' (advanced) level subjects. There can be little doubt he was not university material back then.

At one point he produces yet another fiction (lie) about what happened soon after the murder. This one was created over 26 years after the crime. He claimed on Christmas Day at the Schull swimming event the rumours about him being the murderer were in the air. Presumably being spread by AGS. He has no evidence for this at all. He provides none because it is a lie put out there to support his risible failed narrative of poor little Ian being set up. These sorts of lies would have seen him ripped apart in a witness box. The Police became suspicious of Bailey after seeing his strange statement made on 31.12.1996 and all the false evidence he had supplied.

Most of his narrative in episode 1 on the events of 23.12.96 contradicts many of his previous versions. There are so many. This version directly contradicts what he has written and said in the last couple of years. His narratives contradict him more than any other person. He has zero reliability. No credibility. He was shot. As this book has shown he lies all the time and cannot keep up with those lies. His comments about the three Thomas daughters are so cruel and narcissistic. At every turn, we see how much contempt he had for females.

Jules Thomas and her daughters

Ian Bailey's overbearing narcissism permeates throughout his thankfully short first episode. He is never at fault. He blamed his sister, drink, blamed AGS, blamed organised religion but never blamed himself. In this autobiographical, tour-de-inadequacy' he was terrified of digging deeper into his psyche.

He covers the first 40 years of his life in just over 30 minutes.. His omissions and inclusions are telling. He omits his frequent bedwetting into his teens and his obsession with masturbation and porn from the age of 12. Both indicate potentially deep psychological fissures. Yet a man who says he is committed to the truth misses them out. They point to dark psychological traits and psychosexual inadequacies. These omissions tell us much about him. None of it is good.

Instead, this 66-year-old man finds time to write about the 'womanly needs' of Jules Thomas and wanting some 'nooky' with her. The episode should come with a sick bag. After 9 months of writing, he produces the content of a mirthless carry-on film. This is deeply immature and reduces Jules Thomas to little more than a sexual receptacle and cash machine. That is what he highlights from a relationship lasting 30 years. How shallow can a man get? No expressions of love. Instead, we have "any way we subsequently became entangled". Bailey is allegedly a poet, a wordsmith. Entanglement is a negative experience. It is about things becoming twisted together or caught in a snarl. It is something troublesome. Love plays no part here. It never did with him. He is so shallow and lacking in introspection. He has no empathy and no insight into the human condition. That explained much about his superficial uninspiring poetry.

It gets worse when he comments about the Thomas daughters: Saffy, Virginia, and Fenella. Here we get a front-seat view of his narcissism and misogyny. Approximately 23 minutes into episode 1 he says:

" So, Jules had 3 daughters. The oldest I think was about eighteen at the time, Saffy. She had a 14-year-old called Virginia and a young one called Fenella. And I think they were a little bit jealous of the attention I received from their Mother "

He 'thinks' one was 'about' eighteen while the youngest does not even qualify for an age check. One must keep in mind that he is working from a pre-prepared script. He could be accurate but did not bother to find out. We know from chapter 2 why he knew the exact age of Virginia. She was the 14-year-old he wanted to have sex with. Fenella was born in 1982. She was only a ten-year-old child when he turned up. The ten-year-old would have needed a strong mature caring male role model. She got Bailey.

We had an eighteen-year-old and two children. Their Mother had come through difficult relationships with two men who fathered the girls. Jules was their 'rock'. Yet Bailey the narcissist shows no empathy or compassion. He demonstrated no interest in the challenges these children were facing. In Bailey's world, it is all about him. The only emotion he refers to is jealousy of him. The fears of domestic turbulence, worries about their mother, and concerns about this stranger entering their home are all brushed aside. Poor girls. They had every right to be concerned about him.

There was more than lechery to concern the girls. His treatment of them on the night of one of his brutal and sustained attacks on Jules Thomas is beyond the pale. It is described by Michael Sheridan in his book The Murder of Sophie. It illustrates brilliantly the reasons why the Thomas girls objected to him.

"Bailey had not accompanied her to hospital and the court was told by the defence counsel that when they arrived home, he became hysterical and would not give the keys of the car to the victim's daughter Virginia in an attempt to prevent his severely injured partner being taken to hospital."

"The witness then said he drove the badly injured Thomas to hospital in Cork and when he returned, he agreed to stay in the house in case Bailey might come back and turn his attention to the daughters. He stayed for about three weeks."

Knowing your Mother is being beaten and coerced by a 6' 3" brute is not a source of jealousy but it is a source of anguish, fear, and unhappiness.

Inadvertently Bailey shows us what he really is. He did not know that he was doing it but he did. He showed the listeners he was cold selfish and cruel.

Bailey and his sister

The relationship between a big brother and his little sister can be very loving and endearing. Brothers can often be very protective of their sisters. There can be many memories of those magical moments shared by siblings.

Bailey's abiding 'memory' would appear to be that his little sister was a malignant scheming liar. According to him, his sister told Mrs Bailey lies about him and she was believed. Her sins were so bad that half a century later she felt compelled to apologise to poor, honest victim Ian. The meeting took place in Dublin at a vague unspecified time. Based on what he said it could have been in the middle of the covid pandemic. This is hard to believe. There are no other details. All we are told was it was a mea culpa moment in the presence of the Sainted Ian.

This story is told to set up a key theme that he liked to push. He wanted to portray himself as the victim. He would have people believe that it is others who lie, not him. Anyone with even a slight interest in his life will know he is a pathological liar. A man caught in countless lies.

Is Bailey to be believed? I doubt it. This bullying bedwetting boy. A boy addicted to masturbation and pornography from age 12 in the household. His sister would be seven at the time. Poor little girl being around such a degenerate. It is a sickening scenario. To his death he remained graceless, oafish, and vulgar. He was also a coward who picked on women. Was it any different 50 years ago? Thankfully, the little girl spoke up and her Mother believed her. We can but wonder what the little girl said Bailey was up to. I suspect from early on the family knew Ian 'had issues.

Omissions What Bailey left out of his podcast: Masturbation, pornography, and bedwetting

In his podcast, he tells listeners that he created a puddle of urine on his first day at school aged five. Later he feels the need to tell us that he did not lose his virginity at the age of 16 (why tell us?) What he chose not to tell us about his uncontrolled urinating and sexual obsessions is more interesting.

Interesting because of the things he tried to skate over. On urinating Ian Bailey was enuretic, a bed wetter. This was not restricted to his early school years. It extended long into his teens. As a teenager he would wake up to a urine sodden bed. This behaviour is considered as a potential indication of psychopathy. It certainly may have psychological causes. Bailey tells us nothing. The misdirection of his puddle story is thin gruel in a podcast promising the unvarnished truth. This illustrates a lack of candour and introspection.

Bailey also omits to tell us about his fixation on masturbation and hardcore pornography from the age of twelve. He wrote about it extensively in his diaries and journals. It was something that preoccupied him at least into his early 40's. Did he receive psychiatric or paediatric help as a child in the early 1970's? Once again he is not telling. We know from his writings and social media output that he had an interest in girls under the age of consent. Were his earlier sexual obsessions linked to this predilection?

We don't know because Bailey chose to exclude these significant psychosexual markers. Why does he try and hide them? Why is he so scared of coming clean? We could speculate but, unquestionably, they are important and he lacked the courage to face his psychological demons. Or he knew what it would show and tried to hide it.

In his 44-minute second episode, Bailey attempts to address the complex case. He does so with significant omissions, simplifications, superficiality, and convenient fictions. If you were putting together a legal defence team you would give this self-styled legal academic a wide berth. He had a pitiful grasp of detail and third-rate analytical skills. He was intellectually unfit for the purpose of the second episode.

He claimed Gardai told him paramilitaries would kill him with a bullet to the back of the head if he did not confess to the murder of French victim Sophie Toscan du Plantier. Yet he admits they made no such statement. It was an inference that he chose to make. He was making it up as he went along.

He has spent decades claiming there was some sort of conspiracy to put him behind bars for the murder of Sophie, claiming dark forces were at play. He implied that Police officers were corrupt. What he failed to address in his podcast is that a detailed report by a high-ranking officer (The McAndrew Report) found no evidence for any charges to be taken against a single officer or any disciplinary action. The GSOC 2018 report after several years of investigation had similar findings. The Fennelly Commission led by a High Court Judge and the Jury in a 64-day civil trial in

2014-5iii also found nothing significant to support Bailey's outrageous allegations. Senior officers, Jurors, and leading legal experts are unanimous on no corruption. Yet he, of the no stone unturned claim, chose to ignore the weight of evidence against his conspiracy theory. When the going got tough, Bailey ducked out.

There were further examples of Bailey's abysmal fact-checking. He said "She booked two return tickets - one for Monday, Dec 22, and the other for Christmas Eve. Surely he should know Sunday was the 22nd and Monday was the 23rd. Monday the 23rd being the day Sophie's body was found! Later he states that he was arrested on the 11th of February 1997 when he was arrested on the 10th. This is lazy work by a man who appears to have not mastered his brief. He dishes out slop for his listeners. He could never be trusted on the facts.

He also wrote "A number of Irish passengers noted she appeared to be travelling alone with two suitcases and hand luggage. What appeared to be quite a lot of luggage." He does not tell the listener the source of these statements. He had no idea what the luggage contained. Sophie may have had gifts for people. She may have wanted partially empty cases so she could take gifts back. She may have been taking things over to leave at the house. He wants people to focus on this frippery not evidence. The listener is subjected to speculation of a heavy-drinking man with a poor grasp of the details rather than a rigorous journalist.

In an article written by John Kierans about the second episode of the podcast readers were presented with contradictory versions of events offered by Bailey. The man is no longer capable of keeping his story straight, even within the same article. This is embarrassing. How can a man spend months writing a short script, claim it was forensically detailed, go through a process of 'perfecting', and then produce this confused dross?

During the lengthy podcast, the English journalist says Sophie **did not arrive in Ireland alone** for that final fatal trip to west Cork on December 20 that year.	A number of Irish passengers noted **she appeared to be travelling alone** with two suitcases and hand luggage

Theories and rumours are not facts

For a man who claimed to be fact-orientated, he spent a significant proportion of his time peddling theories and rumours. The whole point of being an investigative journalist is to get to the facts and the truth. Bailey was interested in any narrative that distracted people from the truth. He needed his fantasy world, not reality. He wrote of a theory that Sophie was planning to leave France and her husband and relocate to Ireland. He said she told one West Cork inhabitant she wanted to get away from life in France and start again in Ireland.

Typically, the 'inhabitant' had no name. There is information on when and where this conversation with Sophie took place nor the context of the conversation. He claimed she was moving her possessions over to Ireland.

A further assertion without any grounds. The suggestion she might be doing the moving of possessions a few suitcases at a time is farcical. This sloppy content was the best he could come up with. After a year of 'no stone unturned' research he was peddling these tales. A man who one minute was denouncing ' hearsay' evidence is in the next minute offering unsubstantiated stories from unnamed people as potential fact.

Maybe Bailey had someone else in mind when writing about leaving a country and 'running away ' to West Cork. To get away and start again in Ireland. Someone who could pack their worldly goods into a few suitcases and take off?

At one point he claimed that Sophie Toscan du Plantier had taken haute couture clothing to her cottage that December without any evidence. It is the unfounded speculation of a drunk. This is Bailey presenting fiction rather than detail. He had no time for the findings that show his conspiracy theories were moribund but is happy to offer up empty theories.

Not so much a comedy hour as a comedy second. And not a very funny second at that!

He appeared to have a single 'big comedy idea' for the entire podcast. It was to repeat the words 'defective detective' many times over. Given the things Police officers are called daily by drunken bums and tramps this insult from the Bantry drunk would not have the cut through Bailey imagined. He was a one-trick pony with a very bland trick. After several repetitions, this trick went from bland to banal to boring.

Capability Bailey

In episode 3 of the podcast, Bailey takes time out of his podcast to tell listeners what he had done for Jules at the Prairie. Gardening, building, maintaining dry stone walls, planting flowers and vegetables. general upkeep. He made his help around the cottage sound like he was creating the gardens of a huge country house. He elevates these minor responsibilities to the level of some huge sacrificial endeavour. Most couples earn incomes and do chores around the house. It is what people do. It is not either one thing or the other. His attitude is laughable. He resembles a little boy seeking approval for his derisory efforts. This points to just how lazy he was. For him doing a few basics was a heroic effort. Little wonder he was incapable of doing a full-time paid job.

The claims made by 'Capability Bailey' should not be accepted as fact. Jules Thomas took a very different view. In an interview, she said, «I look after everything here myself; since Ian left nothing much has changed. I think he only mowed the lawn once and he never did the edges. I never let him do the hedges either; he wouldn't know what to cut ". Adding "He would sit out there drinking coffee all day and wine at night; he didn't do much else around here." He was such a fake. He did a few basic things and thought he was putting in a Stakhanovite effort. The man was delusional.

And notice what he did not say. he did not tell us about his efforts to give Jules unconditional love. He did not explain how he tried to help Jules raise her children. No stories about him being a rock for the girls and Jules, a figure of stability. Nothing involving empathy, compassion, personal sacrifice, or tenderness. That was the true Ian Bailey.

Bailey slips up: The Sunday Tribune

Ian Bailey does spend some time in his podcast claiming that on the morning of the murder, he was busy trying to finish an article for the Sunday Tribune as he had a deadline of noon on the 23rd. This was not the story he gave in a statement to AGS on December 31st, 1996. It is yet another example of Bailey changing his story to cover his ass. In his original statements, he said he spent the entire morning 'pottering around' the Prairie cottage. Why the dramatic change? Bailey never explains. This is not the thoroughness he promised, it is a man avoiding uncomfortable truths.

In his new version of events, he says while at the cottage he spoke to the Tribune that morning at around 10.30 am and got an extended deadline to Christmas Eve morning. The problem for Bailey is that the journalists at the paper are clear they did not speak to him that morning or give him an extension. One of the journalists tried calling the cottage but no one picked up. Why does Bailey fail to address these statements and explain them? His selectivity is not honest. These are lies of omission.

The statement of the Tribune journalist is corroborated by the statement of Fenella Thomas who says her mother and Bailey went out for a couple of hours from approximately 10 am – little wonder the call from the Tribune was not answered.

There is further corroboration that he was not at the cottage coming from two highly experienced newspapermen. Dick Cross, and Michael McSweeney both said Bailey told them he had taken photos at the scene of crime between pre 10.30 and 11.30. This was further supported by evidence from husband and wife, vegetable stallholders, who stated that at 11.30 on the 23rd Jules Thomas told them Ian had gone to the crime scene in Dreenane.

Who to believe? The repeatedly lying Ian Bailey or 4 journalists + 2 market traders + Fenella Thomas. He insisted he would deal with everything point by point. He does no such thing. He does not mention the points let alone deal with them.

Bailey also ducked important evidence provided to the French investigators. Saffron Thomas provided a signed statement saying that before noon on 23.12.96 - the day Sophie was murdered- her mother Jules told her about the murder. This was hours before Bailey and Thomas said they found out about the death. Why did Ian 'no stone unturned, 3 law degrees' Bailey completely ignore such details? Why does this get omitted while speculation about dresses is included? Most likely because Saffron's statement points to him being a murderer. While finalising this book it was brought to my attention that there was also a 2002 statement by Saffron Thomas making the same points. There was no excuse for Bailey failing to address this point but there was one explanation. She was telling the truth and he was lying.

Bailey's huge slip up: The Ardamanagh Road incident

The single most significant error made by Bailey in his podcast came when he was giving his version of what Sophie did in Schull on the afternoon of 21.12.1996. He says that Marie Farrell said the man" had subsequently followed the French visitor up the road to her parked car in Ardnamanagh."] The issue was that there was no record of anyone saying that Sophie was followed up on Ardamanagh Road to where her car was parked. No one had ever said Sophie was parked in that area. So, how did he know this information? He was asked about this by the Irish Times for an article on 23.12.2023. He first said

"I did say that in the podcast, and I think it is provable in the statements – I'm sure it's in there in the statements somewhere, so it is provable – I wouldn't be able to put my finger exactly where it is mentioned but I know it is there…"

He was under pressure and rather than go to his notes for the podcast where a reference could be found – if the reference existed - he offered a vague waffly reply. Either there is a statement where it was clearly stated or it was not. Instead, we had 'I think it is provable', 'somewhere', and 'wouldn't be able to put my finger on it'. Typical vague non-answer answers.

Despite that empty fob-off answer, the press seemed happy to give Bailey a free pass. I decided to press on as did a few other members of the public. I pointed out that no such statement existed. Furthermore, if he were not lying when he said he wanted to help Sophie's family then he would specify his source. His rage in his response was palpable and that always made me laugh. Putting to one side his tantrum he then stated that Mary Farrell was on record (saying Sophie was followed to her parked car) and her statement can be found in transcripts. This was a new assertion with the vague suggestion that the information could be found in 'transcripts.'

JPHolzer2021 @JHolzer2021 · Dec 24, 2023 ···

AGS DO not have the statement claimed to exist by Bailey. If he actually cared about the victim he would produce the it. Bailey can't hide all his BS any longer - BUSTED !

5 4 12 734

Ian Kenneth Bailey BCL, LLB, LLM (UCC) ···
@IanKennethBail1

Ye eedgit....MF is on record and her statement can be found in transcripts...ye are such a psychotic ignoramus, so full of Right Wing bigotory and bullshit Hiel Adolph ArseHolzer😂😂😂

5:31 PM · Jan 2, 2024 · **51** Views

This was a standard reply from Bailey. A complete inability to answer straightforward questions combined with rather pitiful attempts at insulting me. I pointed out to him that he had now offered two versions. Both were vague and neither of them gave a specific document. I was not going to let up on this. He needed to be held to account. Soon he came back with version 3. Once again it was, if anything, more vague. It had become 'statements and testimony in Historic case'. The man could not give the reference because it did not exist.

Ian Kenneth Bailey BCL, LLB, LLM (UCC)
@IanKennethBail1

HOLZER IS A FALSE FACE FOR A SICKO....HE SHOULD READ MFS Statements and Testimony in Historic Case...Ye a right fascist langer Arseholzer...Get a life ffs

6:46 PM · Jan 4, 2024 · **112** Views

At this point, he tried to change the whole discussion. He did so with a ploy that was to backfire. It did not work I did not let go. I am sure trying to cover up this huge lie stressed him terribly. He never named the source because it never existed. The fact that he told that story AND tried to 'manufacture' mythical sources in an attempt to cover up what he did, pointed to a man with knowledge that the murderer may have had.

In summary

The loser packed it all in. In 3 amateur episodes, he has demonstrated that he did not know how to make podcasts.

He thought he had a sense of humour, he was wrong. He believed people wanted to hear his dreary monologues, wrong again. He got facts wrong, lied, and showed himself a misogynist and a twisted individual. The big money-making project that would surpass the technical quality of the West Cork podcast and slay the mighty Netflix did not so much start with a bang and go out with a whimper. It started with a whimper and went out with the hissing death rattle of an old broken whoopee cushion.

The In My Own Words podcast is primus inter pares (first among equals) in the pantheon of Bailey flops. The podcast gets top billing because he said it was his gift to posterity. He told us:

- will leave no stone unturned.

- 'It'll be a six-part podcast,' he said. 'The first episode will see me reply to all of the false allegations and nonsense that has been uttered about me over the past 25 years."

- I'm now in a "John Wayne state of mind" and am going to get them back at their own game.'

- "Everything I say will be the truth, the whole truth, and nothing but the truth"

- The final episode will depict the Cork resident's life over the past 12 months, including how his relationship ended, becoming homeless, and 'resurrecting myself again'.

- He will also give listeners the chance to ask, 'reasonable and rational questions' and answer these in the last episode.

- Mr Bailey said he is exploring the possibility of crowd-funding the project online.

- After the podcast is released by the end of this summer, he said he planned to make a documentary about his life. He remarked: 'I've got a very good idea how I want it to turn out and have hours of unused footage that was shot for the Jim Sheridan documentary last year.'

  - He often spoke of him and his 'people' perfecting each episode

He did not quite deliver!

This is comedy gold. a demonstration of what can happen when a hubristic narcissist with limited capabilities talks himself up. Then he has to deliver. Fifteen months later we have 3 tacky, poorly put-together episodes with less than two hours of the spoken word. An utter shambles.

And some of the issues Ian Bailey does not address in his 'rigorous' podcast include:

1. How he knew where to find the dead victim
2. Why he gave a false alibi for the time of the murder to AGS
3. Why did he give AGS a completely false story where he was on the Saturday before the murder
4. Why he has made over 2 dozen significant changes in his statements to AGS about what he was doing between 1 am and 1 pm on 23.12.1996

5. Why most of his statements are uncorroborated and the small bits of corroboration ONLY come from Jules Thomas and her 2 eldest daughters? no one else.
6. Why he has changed his story about the nationality of the victim several times. Why do most of his versions differ from the one he said under oath?
7. Why do the only 3 people who allegedly saw scratches on Bailey before the murder all share the surname Thomas and all were living under the same roof as Bailey.
8. If Bailey were innocent why has he confessed to as many as 12 people?
9. Why has Bailey changed his story of what he did between 11.40 am and 2.40 pm over a dozen times on key points of evidence?
10. Why did he tell two journalists he had photos taken at the scene of the crime before 11.30 am? And why did Jules Thomas tell the Camiers that Bailey was at the scene of the crime at that time?
11. Why did he tell several people that he knew /had met Sophie Toscan du Plantier?
12. Who was his source for claiming Sophie was followed to her car in Schull on 23.12.1996?

These are 12 rational unanswered questions. There are many more avoided by Bailey. This is why he reneged on his promise to answer questions in his last podcast episode. His omission demonstrates his complete inability to address the case against him. The whole project was the embodiment of Ian Bailey. It was dishonest and a shambles.

The malignant narcissist paints himself into a corner

He could not get the date of his arrest right. He always appeared to have little or no grasp of detail. It was why he spent his life being vague and overgeneralising the facts while getting very specific and elaborate regarding his falsehoods. The falsehoods would be made up in the moment and then forgotten in seconds. Lost. To be replaced with new false tales as required by Bailey. Repeatedly lying was the foundation on which the whole Bailey edifice was built, he would lie, repeat lies, and move on. Once his lies were on the record and challenged, everything would start to fall apart and that was what happened.

Bailey called his own bluff when he announced the Podcast. He claimed he would deliver his coup de grâce. He was determined to rebut the case against him. Despite having 3 law degrees and being a former investigative journalist, he could not deliver.

There was no rebuttal. For the last 3 years his tired tropes had been buried. They had been repeatedly challenged and unpicked. He had little left. For years he had dealt in soundbites, rent-a-quote comments, and any theory that came to mind. Now by his assertions, he was going to produce a coherent, tightly argued case, BUT there was no such thing.

His malignant narcissism had painted him into a corner.

There were books, press articles and I had written dozens of detailed blogs dismantling his flimsy defence. He could no longer try and hide behind the case made by the DPP, no one took that seriously. He had talked a good game. He claimed he would shock people with his revelations. It was all hot air.

He managed 3 episodes running to less than two hours. Much of it tedious waffle about his childhood. What remained was a shambles. There was not a single press article extolling the virtues of the podcast. No one praised some case-cracking insight from Bailey, there were none. It was a damp squib. He had failed.

It was worse than neutral. He had made many mistakes that pointed to his culpability. His vain belief that he could dig himself out of his problems had resulted in him digging himself into a deeper hole. He had brought this upon himself. It was sublime. By the end of it – even if he did not declare it – he knew he had failed. He could not defend himself and everyone saw it. This was a crushing defeat for Bailey. His boasts of mass downloads and positive feedback did not con people into seeing him as a success. They saw a loser desperately lying to cover his failure.

He had exhausted himself in his war against reality. He was broken by the truth. A few months after his final episode the overwhelming stress of his defeat led to a series of heart attacks. He had become a dead man walking. He was completely defeated. There was no way back. He had lost. He was lost.

That would be his legacy for posterity.

CHAPTER **9**

Tik Tok Tik Tok

In the long drawn-out saga of his legacy podcast, Bailey kept on changing his launch deadline. Even he had started to notice that things had been dragging on for an age. He was becoming even more of a laughingstock than normal. Each new delay was met with derision.

I suspect in a brief moment of sobriety he realised that he needed to act. This was his moment to stand tall, face the challenge square on, and deal with it. The whole project was teetering on the brink. He would have to draw upon his recent decades of experience. The piss ups, the drugs, the crap poetry, the carving of wooden penises, and being the designer of the third best Moob T-shirt in the greater Bantry area 2023. He came up with a stupid story that blamed someone else, never him, and told the world through a brief TIKTOK video.

> **MARCH 2023 Family tragedy**
>
> "Hi there so, friends fans and followers, um , a quick podcast update, unfortunately my sound engineer who's been recording the episodes has had a family tragedy and it's taken him away from the case, and that's why nothing has come out but it will do."

There it was. he could now relax. The crisis had been averted, or at least delayed for a short while. The unnamed engineer had a completely unspecified family tragedy at an unknown time. It would go on presumably for an unspecified period. Though a tragedy, he did not send the engineer and the victim of the tragedy his best wishes or condolences.

The rumour at the time was that the sound engineer had not been paid and there was little prospect of him getting money any time soon. He was understandably digging his heels in. No money then no finalised recordings. While continuing to brag about having money it was obvious Bailey was skint. He had been observed dipping in bins for food and trying to persuade people in bars to buy him drinks. This perception was supported by later TIKTOK videos in which he is sitting in a darkened room in an overcoat, scarf, and hat. As he speaks it is so cold you can see his breath. Apparently, he had no money for heating. I feel sure that had he been challenged about his visible breath Bailey would have claimed it was a cryogenic business opportunity that he was exploring.

With no payments made it is likely the engineer pulled the pin and Bailey was left up the swanee without a podcast. Certainly, anyone listening to his podcast would not fail to notice its appalling production values. Plenty of changing background noise, inept cutting , a total absence of music or professional links. It gave every impression of being recorded on a PC with basic recording facilities in a bedsit late at night.

If Bailey had re-recorded the episodes then the family tragedy story was a fabrication. It was a lie told by a desperate man. That is where my money would be. What about you? So far, so bad. Approximately three weeks later he posted another TIKTOK video about the delay in the podcast. Bailey told his public.

> **APRIL 2023 Motorcycle accident**
>
> "Hi, so um, the reason the podcast hasn't come out is my sound engineer Mark has had a very nasty motorcycle accident, and at the moment is incapacitated, he's got the master tapes and I'm, I'm, a bit banjaxed."

You would have to have a heart of stone not to feel for poor Mark the sound engineer. So, with my stony heart, let me explain why I did not shed any tears for Mark. I think Bailey was lying. If you have read to this point in the book and do not share that conclusion, you may wish to flick through it again.

My immediate reaction was he had completely forgotten about his family tragedy story. He probably recorded it when drunk and now does not remember doing it. However, the external pressure is getting to the narcissist so he unknowingly responds similarly. He produced a second vague story that blamed someone else, not himself, and told the world through a brief TIKTOK video. There was however a twist in the second case. The second time around poor Ian became a 'poor me' victim. Okay, Mark had a very nasty motorcycle accident but Ian was banjaxed! In the victimhood top trumps world of Bailey being banjaxed is worse than being mangled on a motorbike.

Picture the scene. Mark is in an induced coma in an intensive care unit. His broken limbs have been wired back together. A body held together by stitches; medications being dripped into his body. The loud beeping of machines does not awaken him. Then his eyes suddenly open and he struggles to free himself. The alarms go off and a team of doctors and nurses rush to his aid and they try to hold him in place. Mark wanted to speak and a nurse briefly removed the oxygen mask. Gasping for breath Mark speaks

"Is Ian okay?…has he been banjaxed?"

Two nurses exchanged glances.

"He is fine. Not a banjaxed bone in his body."

Mark relaxed. They replaced the oxygen mask and checked all the drips were connected. In a moment he was fast asleep. One of the nurses whispered to her colleague

"Of course, poor Mr Bailey was banjaxed….and all because of this bastard."

Two versions

This was a case of two versions in a matter of weeks. Bailey had forgotten his initial false excuse and come up with a similar one. I raised this conflict of stories with him. Naturally, when caught out, he retreated neither confirming nor denying my observation. He did this all the time so I thought little of it. It was just another example of him lying to everybody.

When doing some research for this book I was going to include this example in either a 'Bailey is a liar' chapter or 'Bailey makes a hopeless podcast chapter.' I discovered that the family crisis story had been removed. This was unusual for the old sop. One might even say he was being cunning. Dishonest but cunning. I imagined that he was contented that he had pulled a fast one and covered his embarrassment. Unfortunately for him, he had extremely limited technology savvy. There are many free online programmes for downloading TIKTOK videos. I had copies of both of his excuse videos.

This development doubled his woes. First, he had told these highly unbelievable tales. And second, he had stealthily removed one of them. If both were true, no matter how improbable why would he remove one? He had caught himself in his machinations. He was no master manipulator. He was a confused dishonest man.

In the final chapter, I will reveal my correspondence with Ian Bailey for the first three weeks of 2024. His last three weeks. Here, I will share some relevant extracts on the double TIKTOK excuses. In an email to him on January 18th, I mentioned the bizarre conflicting videos he had sent to his followers. There was no reply using any medium.

JAN 18th Give us a hand

Hi Baileybobs

fair do's you've been exposed re Ardamanagh Rd . We are just too clever for you.

I am doing a comedy chapter for my book on the absolute farce that was you podcast. I am tidying up a bit about some of your excuses for taking 9 months 22 days to deliver a meagre 33.55 mins episode 1.

On Tik tok in late March you attribute the podcast delay to a family tragedy for Mark the sound engineer. But in early April you then claim it was due to Mark having a nasty motorcycle accident. When i pointed out your lies the March video disappeared.

As you can see (attached) I have copies of both (along with other stuff you deleted). To be clear is it your contention that the family tale is a barefaced lie and (i am chuckling here) the life threatening accident is the truth 😂 😂.

I must say that your inability to pull on your big boy pants and answer my questions works well in my book.

Chins up old lad

JP

Jan 21ˢᵗ those tik tok thingumies
Ian mate,

the response to me putting up your two Tik Toks about Mark's miseries has been very encouraging. It has been a gift to me. so much so that i will now dedicate a short chapter to it in my book.

Bailey received the 21.01.2024 email just over an hour before he died. Throughout January 2024 he had been asked about debating the facts of the case, Ardamanagh Rd, his ludicrous claims of newfound wealth, and his TIKTOK lie and on the 21st his paedophilic inclinations were mentioned. He was being crushed under his lies.

It was the truth with which he could not cope.

CHAPTER 10

The Holzer Bailey letters

From late 2023 I started work on this book. The aim was always to show how social media shone a light on Ian Bailey's character and preferences. The book also shows how he was challenged and ridiculed in an attempt to counteract his long-term vileness. The weight of the evidence was getting too much for the man.

On December 23rd, 2023 an article in the Irish Times, by Barry Roche, reported the views of Sophie's uncle. The focus was on comments made by Ian Bailey in his own podcast, He stated that on 21.12.96 a man followed Sophie up Ardamanagh Rd to where her car was parked. This was something I had written about in summer 2023. There has never been a single statement saying a man followed Sophie to her parked car that day. He had made a mistake.

I decided to press Bailey hard on this topic. I was not alone. I would do so via social media, an upcoming podcast, emails, and leafleting if that were required. The aim was simple, get him to specify his source. Often he would fob people off. This time the aim was to keep pressing him until he gave a testable answer. Under pressure, he offered three separate explanations. None of them were true, all of them ridiculously vague. He had no answer. People would not let up. This book and Ardamanagh Road would become the focus of my interactions with Bailey in 2024.

From the beginning, I made it clear to Bailey that I would stop sending him emails if he asked me to do so. If he pointed out anything I had got factually wrong I would remove it. He never replied via email. Instead, he responded in his way through social media.

This formed the basis of the Holzer-Bailey letters. Not quite Zelda and Scott Fitzgerald or Sigmund Freud and Carl Jung but interesting all the same.

Dec 31st Podcast

Now then Ian,

I will be doing the first of my 'podcast appearances early in 2024 with Ian Dynamo Kelly - you did a podcast with him a while back.

I told him I would happily be on it with you with him in the chair. I did say I thought you would chicken out as you know you are incapable of debating me. You prefer to hide and tweet little boy insults.

We could bottom out your lack of a source for your Ardamanagh road story / you could clarify all your lies in my nemesis analysis / explain all the material showing you have a sexual interest in underage girls / your lies about a woman being a convicted sex worker.

I think you have not got the balls for it. I will read this email out in the podcast to show that you had the chance but bottled it.

Chins up

JPH

JAN 1ST PODCAST

Ian

then its a no. I will make sure everyone knows you bottled it

JPH

Bailey's response

Ian Kenneth Bailey BCL, LLB, LLM (UCC)
@IanKennethBail1

Ye eedgit....MF is on record and her statement can be found in transcripts...ye are such a psychotic ignoramus, so full of Right Wing bigotory and bullshit Hiel Adolph ArseHolzer😂 😂 😂

5:31 PM · Jan 2, 2024 · **913** Views

🗨 3   ↻   ♡   🔖

JAN 2nd FIRING BLANKS

Hey up old lad this has been passed to me. You are funny and very, very scaredy

Ian Kenneth Bailey BCL, LLB, LLM (UCC)
@IanKennethBail1

HOLZER IS A FALSE FACE FOR A SICKO....HE SHOULD READ MFS
Statements and Testimony in Historic Case...Ye a right fascist langer
Arseholzer...Get a life ffs

6:46 PM · Jan 4, 2024 · **6,902** Views

○ 7   ⟲ 2   ♡ 3   🔖   ⬆

Too scared to debate me live. I will give that tweet
a mention in the upcoming podcasts. Not even in the
Sheridan documentary does dozy Farrell spew out your
Ardamanagh Rd story and the parked car. So funny watching
you floundering. Wandering around Bantry like a tramp.
Give me more of your lil boy jibes for my book.

JPH

From Bailey January 4th

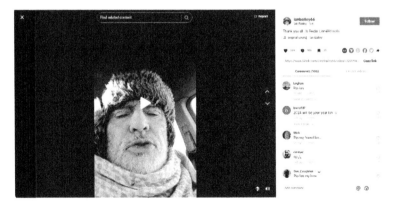

JAN 4th POOR LAMB

Now then Ian,

first you said your Ardmanagh Road story in the podcast was based on the statements THEN

second you attributed it to a statement 'in a transcript' THEN

third you say "MFS statements and testimony in historic case" You are obviously struggling. This is a surprise given your legal training and journalistic background.

Try giving a specific detailed answer. Name the document and date it. Provide direct quotations of the content.. Otherwise, you appear to be flapping around like some old drunk. If it helps to call me names , do so. Those tweets will go in my book. So funny.

So Ian T...R...Y A...N...D B..E S..P..E C..I..F..I..C

We're not going to stop til you do. HTH

Chop chop mate.

From Bailey TIKTOK and Twitter January 6th

Ian Bailey posted a TIKTOK video stating that he had enjoyed a record financial year and it was all due to me. He wanted to talk himself up while denigrating me.

I knew he was skint and this was a response to all the pressure I was putting on him re Ardamanagh Rd.

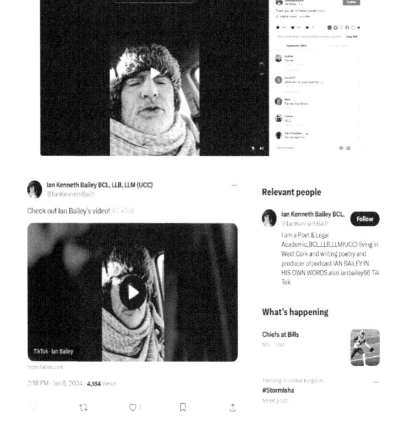

Jan 6TH IDEAL FOR MY BOOK

Now then Ian
the tik tok video - brilliant

You could not have done much more in under a minute to confirm several of the points I make about you in my book. that I am inside your head even though you block me, that you are terrified of having an open debate with me. This results in you continuing to tell lies about your success 😂. Have you forgotten that people see you and photograph you walking around Bantry like a tramp living on scraps 😂. That here is yet another example of Ian Bailey making grandiose claims while completely unable to prove any of it.

You are the shout out 'king' who does not do shout outs. Its a hoot.

Stills and transcript content from your video will go in my book . Cheers.

Now about your silly unverified tale re Ardamanagh Rd. Have you managed to locate the transcripts (dated) and the actual content. You really are struggling old lad. I will mention it in the podcast.

Please let me have more of you schoolboy drivel, its priceless.

Chins up

JPH

From Bailey late January 6th

Ian Kenneth Bailey BCL, LLB, LLM (UCC)
@IanKennethBail1

Did anybody here of the excremention of Fascist Pyhsco Dudearelist JPHolzer of Yorkshire Anti Neurotic Feaces… 😂 😂 😂

11:16 PM · Jan 6, 2024 · **5,973** Views

⟲ 2   ♡ 1   🔖   ↥

Jan 7 th AIM UP LAD

Matey

are you okay? I thought I would send you a few tips.

The tik tok video
If you are claiming to have had the best year yet -

1. Don't shuffle around Bantry dressed as a dirty tramp
2. Don't push an old supermarket trolley around like those USA vagrants
3. Don't stink out charity shops
4. Don't urinate in shop doorways
5. Wear clean, ironed clothes
6. have a proper wash.
7. If you are going to make a video announcing your success do not appear in a stained crappy scarf, do something about your skin and replace that rancid hat,
8. Don't do the video seated in a poxy old car. That really is rather low rent,

9. Try and have some proof of what you say. I have helped people realise that you like to make big claims but you can never back them up

10. Making big claims with no back up results in you looking desperate.

Moving on thanks for the late night tweet. That will go in the foreword of the book it illustrates your anal fixation, incoherence and that when you tell people you ignore me you are, yet again, lying. Its got the lot. Cheers.

Did that tweet appear lucid inside your head? If it did seek medical assistance old lad.

While I am here, can you give us the precise source or sources you used for the Ardamanagh Road part of your podcast. The source / date recorded and the actual content. Enough of the inane blather. We will not quit on this . I doubt ASSOPH will quit on this. If we need to we will even do a leaflet campaign in Bantry. Time to stop digging Ian. Face up.

JPH

Jan 8TH CRACK ON

Hi matey

so !

Not a word in all the original statements by MF about 5'8" / French beret/ following Sophie up the road / following her to where her car was parked.. She contradicts many of the points you made..

So you are buggered there.

Then we have -

1. 2011 evidence to the French - 5'8" tick Follows Sophie tick here a flat hat and no following to a parked car !
2. MATC 2021 no height,, no headwear , goes up the road behind her, no following to a parked car.

Neither of those say what you said and of course MF is already riddled with major contradictions.

In which statement does she say French beret and follows Sophie to her parked car? On 3 occasions you have referred to having seen written docs that confirm what you said.. What are they? Why can't you just name them? Crack on lad,

If you think this is bad, wait til you see our next paper and one statement from 2011 that blows you away.

Tis such fun.

JPH

Bailey January 9th

My responses to Bailey's ridiculous video were not what he expected so he moved on to his favourite ploy, a press article. He wanted the article to support the themes of his video. It backfired and caused people to enjoy some of my replies and laugh at Bailey. The man was at an end.

COURTS

'KEEP IT UP' | Ian Bailey thanks 'number one Twitter troll' for best ever financial year

"Well done, keep up the abuse "

SUNDAY WORLD

"Yes Ian I hope you have another killer of a year," wrote another. "This guy was made to be a scapegoat," wrote one.

"France would love for you to pay them a visit," wrote another.

The person who is playing the role of 'troll' in the online disagreement posted their own tweets in response:

"Bantry's best known tramp Bailey is in full cry baby mode on fb. Someone call UC Hospital, Ian is either back on the drink or his medications need adjusting - just look at this...he thinks that is coherent and funny. Oh dear."

SUNDAY WORLD

Sinead O'Connor and Ian Bailey

"Alexa show me that I have residence inside Ian Bailey's head?" the user added.

The person running the account states "Send Ian Bailey to France. May he never return to Ireland or the UK," and has an image of Mrs Toscan du Plantier as their profile picture.

Jan 9th SUNDAY WORLD

Matey
just seen the Sunday World piece. Great for my book that.
Shows how rattled you are about Ardmananagh Road , as you
should be, that was a costly slip.
My favourite message re the article was - dirty spaced out
beggar claims he is in the money,.

Tee He

JPH

https://m.sundayworld.com/crime/courts/ian-bailey-thanks-
number-one-twitter-troll-for-best-ever-financial-year/
a2112202197.html

Jan 10 th IAN BAILEY to Welfare

Dear Sir or Madam,

in recent days Ian Kenneth Bailey aged 66 has taken to
publicly announcing his financial success during 2023.
Good luck to him. If he is to be believed then he should
require fewer benefits. I hope you will be able to check just
how must the state can now retain.
As an academic lawyer I feel sure he has kept you fully
informed. As a courtesy I have copied in Mr Bailey.

Please find links to his recent tiktok announcement and press article re his new riches.

Kind Regards

JP

Tik Tok announcement

https://www.tiktok.com/@ianbailey66/video/7320998604695440673?

January 14th Small social media campaign

Bailey had given three vague answers to the Ardanamanagh Road question. He has then added his standard distraction technique found in his January 6th TIKTOK and the related press article on the 9th. This would normally guarantee that a topic had been buried. It was not. My email on the 9th told him the issue was not going away. On the 14th the message below was tweeted hundreds of times by many posters. It was a clear message to him that this issue was live.

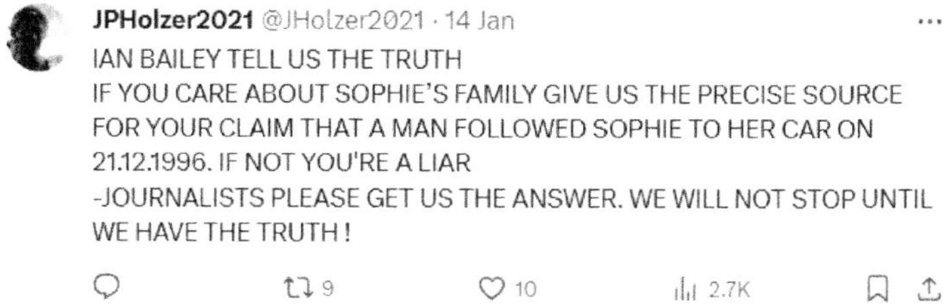

JPHolzer2021 @JHolzer2021 · 14 Jan

IAN BAILEY TELL US THE TRUTH
IF YOU CARE ABOUT SOPHIE'S FAMILY GIVE US THE PRECISE SOURCE FOR YOUR CLAIM THAT A MAN FOLLOWED SOPHIE TO HER CAR ON 21.12.1996. IF NOT YOU'RE A LIAR
-JOURNALISTS PLEASE GET US THE ANSWER. WE WILL NOT STOP UNTIL WE HAVE THE TRUTH !

9 10 2.7K

The email on the 14th told Bailey about the campaign and how if he refused to offer honest answers there would be flyers and posters to follow.

Jan 14 ARDAMANAGH ROAD

Matey
today we are starting off with a small campaign aimed at getting you to provide the exact source for your claim a man in a French beret followed Sophie to her car on 21.12.1996.

You keep ducking the issue. We will not quit. Flyers and poster to follow.

If you cannot answer you are a liar and it then would appear that YOU followed Sophie.

IAN BAILEY TELL US THE TRUTH

IF YOU CARE ABOUT SOPHIE'S FAMILY GIVE US THE PRECISE SOURCE FOR YOUR CLAIM THAT A MAN FOLLOWED SOPHIE TO HER CAR ON 21.12.1996. IF NOT YOU'RE A LIAR

-JOURNALISTS PLEASE GET US THE ANSWER. WE WILL NOT STOP UNTIL WE HAVE THE TRUTH !

Just give us the answer mate,

JPH

JAN 18th Give us a hand

Hi Baileybobs

fair do's you've been exposed re Ardamanagh Rd . We are just too clever for you.

I am doing a comedy chapter for my book on the absolute farce that was you podcast. I am tidying up a bit about some of your excuses for taking 9 months 22 days to deliver a meagre 33.55 mins episode 1.

On Tik tok in late March you attribute the podcast delay to a family tragedy for Mark the sound engineer. But in early April you then claim it was due to Mark having a nasty motorcycle accident. When i pointed out your lies the March video disappeared.

As you can see (attached) I have copies of both (along with other stuff you deleted). To be clear is it your contention that the family tale is a barefaced lie and (i am chuckling here) the life threatening accident is the truth 🤣🤣.

I must say that your inability to pull on your big boy pants and answer my questions works well in my book.

Chins up old lad

JP

[Attached were the TIKTOKs I tweeted out the same day]

On the 18^{th of} January I tweeted the conflicting TIKTOKs put out by Bailey to explain the podcast delays Now there was still Ardamanagh Rd, his lying about his financial success and lies about his engineer.

Jan 21st those tik tok thingumies

Ian mate,

the response to me putting up your two Tik Toks about Mark's miseries has been very encouraging. It has been a gift to me. so much so that i will now dedicate a short chapter to it in my book.

As you are the focus of the book and in a spirit of Christian caring I thought I would share with you the progress on the "In his own words" chapters. It is sooo funny. Have you any idea how many times you changed the launch date for episode 1? How many times you were incapable of providing a specific date rather than 'end of the month' 'January or February'. When you see all the examples from press interviews, Tik Tok and Twitter it screams FARCICAL. Add to that the changes in the duration of episodes, the number of episodes and the content of episodes it reinforces the impression of a man out of his depth.

And then after all that the 'perfected'(sic) recordings are dreadful. Mediocre sound quality, some risible cutting and the absence of basic elements expected in podcasts. You get dates wrong, you contradict yourself and then there are the major slip ups like Sophie being followed to her parked car. That is not the only example!

Your omissions about your frequent nocturnal emissions (see what I did there) and childhood interest in porn and masturbating are left out. Poor Brenda. Entering your bedroom each morning wondering what you had done to those frequently scrubbed sheets,

I think next I will send you the details of your on the record sexual interest in underage girls in the 1990s right through last year. We can both agree I am a fair minded man who follows the facts. If I have made a factual error let me know. and I will make changes. Be assured that the image of the 'naughty girl' masturbating that you so liked, and the dick pic of your unimpressive penis will be redacted for taste.

I love the way we communicate. I write to you and then you run to Tik Tok, Twitter, the press and vent your spleen.

Pip pip

Keep your chins up

JP

Not so much with a bang but a whimper

"Do not go gentle into that good night,
Old age should burn and rave at close of day;
Rage, rage against the dying of the light."

Dylan Thomas

His last communication directed towards me was the January 9th newspaper article. It joined the Shattered Lives Podcast on the short list of media coverage that Bailey made no reference to and refused to publicise. It backfired terribly.

Subsequent sightings of him before he died painted a picture of a broken man, aged beyond his years, shuffling around a town that did not want him. The final email was sent to Ian Bailey at 12.20 on the 21st of January. At approximately 13.30 he collapsed close to his temporary home. Some twisted Bailey supporters claim that the paedophilic murderer was hounded to his death by a group of trolls. A ludicrous suggestion. The people who challenged Bailey challenged his repeated lies, including the ones he told about the murder of Sophie. They challenged the lies that supported the false persona presented by Bailey. They called out his bullying and threatening of women.

The reality was Bailey was confronted by the truth and he could not live with it. The truth did for Bailey. How apt. After his death, the press reports showed us that Bailey had died a friendless, impoverished, and bitter man. (Appendix 3)

Bailey said he loved the poetry of 'fellow Welshman' Dylan Thomas. Poor Ian, No burning, no rave. No rage against the dying of the light. A reviled drunken tramp collapsed, dead, in a gutter and no one cared.

Good riddance.

Appendix 1

The chronology of Ian Bailey's involvement in the Sophie Toscan du Plantier case

December 23rd 1996: The battered dead body of Sophie Toscan du Plantier is found close to her home in Dreenane in Co Cork.

January 1997: Marie Farrell contacted gardaí saying she had seen a man acting suspiciously at Kealfadda Bridge, close Sophie's home, in the early morning of December 23. She later identified the man as Ian Bailey, a local man.

February 1997: Ian Bailey was arrested, questioned, and released without charge.

January 1998: Ian Bailey was re-arrested, questioned, and released without charge.

December 2003/Jan 04: Ian Bailey took a civil case against seven newspapers for linking him to the killing. He lost five of the actions. He won two, but these two were not linked to Sophie but the claim he had assaulted his former wife.

October 2005: Marie Farrell withdrew her statements that she had seen Bailey at Kealfadda Bridge. She claimed she had been pressurised by gardaí.

May 2007: Assistant Commissioner Ray McAndrew recommended to DPP that there was insufficient evidence to support claims by Bailey and others against members of AGS. DPP found no grounds for any prosecutions.

July 2008: After a new investigation was set up in France, Sophie Toscan du Plantier's body was exhumed for a fresh autopsy. The investigation was headed up by Judge Patrick Gachon. Back in Ireland, the DPP recommended that no prosecution follow from the Garda probe into the withdrawal of Marie Farrell's statements.

March 2011: As the French investigation continued, a High Court ruling in Ireland cleared the way for Ian Bailey's extradition to France.

October 2011: French investigators interviewrd up to 30 people as part of their fresh probe.

November 2011: The Supreme Court heard an application by Ian Bailey for a fresh High Court hearing.

March 2012: The Supreme Court unanimously granted Bailey's appeal.

August 2013: After a successful civil case was brought in France by Sophie Toscan du Plantier's family, they were awarded damages of €150,000. Under French law, victims of crime can sue the state for damages.

March 2015: Ian Bailey was unsuccessful when he took a civil action against the State and gardaí. After a trial of over

60 days the Jury needed only two hours to reject the claims of Bailey. During the trial Marie Farrell, Bailey's 'star witness' stormed out of the witness box while being cross examined.

January 2016: A new judge was appointed to oversee the French investigation, after Judge Gachon was promoted.

April 2018: An unsuccessful challenge was made by Ian Bailey in the French Supreme Court against French efforts to put him on trial for the murder.

August 2018: The Garda Síochána Ombudsman Commission found that there was no clear evidence of high-level corruption by gardaí investigating the murder, This showed Bailey's claims of corrupt and criminal behaviour by AGS were without merit

May 2019: A French trial in the absence of Ian Bailey got underway in Paris. It found him guilty in his absence and imposed a 25-year sentence.

October 2020: The High Court ruled that Mr Bailey would not be extradited to France. It was made clear that the decision was not based on the guilt or innocence of Bailey.

April 2021: Mr Bailey and his long-term partner, Jules Thomas, split up after almost three decades together. She demanded that he leave her property.

June 2022: Gardaí announced a cold case review into the murder in Ireland.

December 2022: Gardaí held a press conference in Schull where they called for further witnesses to come forward to help their investigation. Officers said they wished to speak to any person who met, spoke with, or had any interaction with Ms du Plantier from when she arrived in Ireland on December 20, 1996, to when her body was discovered on the morning of December 23.

January 2024: Ian Bailey died. The cold case review continues.

Appendix 2

Responding to Bailey's spurious activities and turning the screw and his standard reply

One of the further ways selected to put pressure in Ian Bailey was to challenge the narrative that he was keen to push. Regrettably, too many journalists were content to print whatever he said. Rarely was he asked tough questions in these articles. So a group of private citizens, me included, tried to hold Bailey's feet to the fire. Tactically he should have ignored us. However, his arrogance and desire to be in the public light compelled him to try and hit back. He was being brought down by his personality flaws.

The aim was always the same. To keep challenging Bailey's faulty narrative and to unsettle him with jibes and wind ups.

JPHolzer2021 @JHolzer2021 · 17m · · ·
"He has repeatedly denied involvement in the killing."
And he has repeatedly confessed
And he has repeatedly lied to the Police including offering a false alibi. /6

JPHolzer2021 @JHolzer2021 · 13m · · ·
" It's astonishing that we still do not know what will happen next."
we? Bailey does not know and it is none of his business. It really upsets him
that he has nothing but his own fakery.
THEY know and Bailey has to suck it up. - Don't you matey. /7

JPHolzer2021 @JHolzer2021 · 10m · · ·
"Bailey said it was clear the French were determined to hold him
responsible."
Well duuuur matey ! Three Judges presided over a trial. They went thru all
the evidence and YOU were found guilty. (drum roll) ...You are responsible.
HTH /8

JPHolzer2021 @JHolzer2021 · 5m · · ·
"Technically, I'm an international fugitive. The French are still trying to get
me. "
Wrong. Legally you are guilty of murder, virtually all bar Ireland would
extradite you in a heartbeat. You're not the victim, stop whimpering, you're
the murderer and the French will have you /9

JPHolzer2021   · · ·
@JHolzer2021

Replying to @JHolzer2021, @Cmused13705 and @MarkennethBart

" It doesn't keep me awake at night"
This is what comes of drinking yourself unconscious at
night.
/10

12:03 am · 12 Apr 2022 · Twitter Web App

View Tweet analytics

Tweet your reply

JPHolzer2021 @JHolzer2021 · 27s · · ·
Replying to @JHolzer2021, @Cmused13705 and @MarkennethBart
"But until it's over, it's not over."

You're damn right its not 👍 /11

Bailey's typical reply – lying, threatening, and running to the police

aggressive on the aul keyboard is

Ian Kenneth Bailey
@IanKennethBail1

Replying to @JHolzer2021 and @Chris98133703

Your a nasty little runt.. Reporting you to Irish and UK authorities... You should consider the effects of you prosecution on your poor wife, child and dog. You gave yourself away... Retribution for being a total Arseholzer is coming your way

8:33 · 12 Apr 22 · Twitter for Android

Appendix 3

A selection of newspaper quotes about Ian Bailey immediately after his death

The Sun UK Oliver Harvey 22.01.2024

"He was supposed to get in shape for a triple heart bypass, but the world's most famous murder suspect nevertheless hit the bottle and the smokes as if every day was his last. "

"Bailey was terrified Irish police were about to rearrest him for the murder of glamorous filmmaker Sophie Toscan du Plantier."

"Like every functioning psychopath, Ian Bailey was an adept liar."

"Ian Bailey died with little or no money and had not made a will."

"was due to be evicted within weeks as his landlord was selling the building."

"regularly got annoyed at various people generating large amounts of money from the du Plantier case via books, podcasts and television."

"It is infuriating because I have hardly any money and am living week to week just to survive."

The Irish Sun John Kierans 26.01.2024

"Never used the bedroom which just had a mattress on it."

"He slept every night on the couch with his feet on wooden pallets placed at the end of it."

"The place was like an absolute tip."

"There were a huge number of files on his case, plus hundreds of notebooks everywhere, bags of rubbish and empty bottles."

"The flat was also full of wooden penises, believe or not, which for some strange reason he carved and would try to sell in the local markets…"

"He was forever writing things about people in his notebooks, especially those he hated…He would write things down and say he was putting a curse on them."

"Bailey had a public reputation as a bit of a ladies man but the friend said he wasn't."

"I think he found it really difficult to look after himself after he split with Jules."

"He really had a very sad ending."

Evoke.ie Mary Carr 28.01.2024

" There was no one at Ian Bailey's cremation except funeral staff."

The Irish Sun Lauren Kelly 28.01.2024

"There was an air about him that was resigned. He told me a couple of times: "I'm going to die, the end is near." Jim Sheriden

"He died of a bad heart, brought on by excessive drinking and smoking, but there was no doubt he had post-traumatic stress from all of this." Jim Sheriden

Irish Mirror John Kierans 04.02.2024

"It is understood he often dressed up as a woman and partly exposed himself to male crew members in a handful of the scenes as a 'joke'".

"He often dressed up as a woman for fun. I always thought he was gay because he was more interested in men than women."

"He would record most days when he was bored and talked for hours if he was drunk."

Printed in Great Britain
by Amazon

40802880R00126